The Right to Privacy in India

The Right to Privacy in India

Concept and Evolution

Authored by
Gaurav Goyal

Co-Authored and edited by
Dr. Ravinder Kumar

PARTRIDGE
A Penguin Random House Company

To order additional copies of this book, contact
Partridge India
000 800 10062 62
orders.india@partridgepublishing.com

www.partridgepublishing.com/india

Contents

ACKNOWLEDGEMENT

This book is based on the early concept and subsequent evolution of the Right to Privacy in India. I am grateful to a number of people, without the efforts and inputs of those; this book would not have materialized.

First and foremost, I would like to thank (Retd.) Mr. Justice D. Murugesan for sharing his knowledge and the invaluable inputs with me.

I am grateful to my father for being encouraging and supportive in all my endeavors.

Finally, I am grateful to my family and friends for their eternal support without which this book would not have seen the light of day.

-Gaurav Goyal

ACKNOWLEDGEMENT

I am grateful to Mr. Akshit Goyal, Student, The West Bengal National University of Juridical Sciences, Kolkata, for the valuable contribution he made as a researcher for the book. He also helped me in editing the book.

I am also grateful my family for their eternal support without which this book would not have seen the light of day.

-Dr. Ravinder Kumar

Preface

The phenomenon that the individual shall have full protection in person and in property is a principle as old as the common law; but it has been found necessary from time to time to define the exact nature and extent of such protection. Political, social, and economic changes entail the recognition of new rights. Thus, in very early times, the law gave a remedy only for physical interference with life and property, for trespasses *vi et armis*. Then the "right to life" served only to protect the subject from battery in its various forms; liberty meant freedom from actual restraint; and the right to property secured to the individual his lands and his cattle. Later, came recognition of man's spiritual nature, of his feelings and his intellect. Gradually the scope of these legal rights broadened; and now the right to life has come to mean the right to enjoy life, -- the right to be let alone; the right to liberty secures the exercise of extensive civil privileges; and the term "property" has grown to comprise every form of possession -- intangible, as well as tangible.[1]

Personal Liberty which to some extent is also termed as privacy is a dynamic and evolving concept. The realm of

---

[1] These principles were laid down by brandies warren in the 19th century.

this right is expanding and is under constant supervision as the society and the culture grows.

The purpose of penning down this book the constant development of the right to personal space i.e. personal liberty or privacy and to analyze the changing dimension of the right guaranteed under article 21 of the Indian Constitution. The right under Article 21 is available to every citizen regardless of which class, section of society he or she belongs to.

The realm of personal liberty has been extended to include the well organized legal education, with specialization in different branches of law, through the adequate number of law colleges with proper infrastructure including expert law teachers and staff, like our own college for example. Such a development has given the required personal space to every student to grow as a student and also a human being and to realize the value of every right guaranteed under the constitution and how relevant it is to the society.

In this book we have tried to compare the present day scenario with what was followed during the times of Ramayana and Mahabharata and also the rules of arthshastra in light of present day statutes.

In the past several years, invasions of privacy by the news media have become a routine part of the coverage of public figures. At the same time, this type of news gathering and reporting has come under increasing criticism by the news audience as well as by media critics. Questions are raised about the appropriateness and purpose of revealing information the subjects of such reports would prefer to keep private. Competing claims are made about the importance and value of privacy, on the one hand, and the public's desire and need to know, on the other. What is needed is a way to compare these competing claims in the evaluation of invasions of privacy that is grounded in fundamental ethical concepts and principles. In this study three models are provided for the ethical analysis of privacy invasion by the news media. The models are described generally and thereafter specifically applied to news reporting which invades the privacy of public figures.

I have carefully structured my topic to "The Right to Privacy: Does it give the right to invade someone's privacy and the jurisprudence behind the right."

I have tried to compare the right to privacy in respect of several problems that a man faces day to day. Also I feel that this is important for me, because the society that we live in has a constant habit of invading one's privacy without any authorized channel or prior permission.

Every day, we come across cases, at least I do, where the private space of either the parents or the children is invaded by either of the two, if this is not enough then we have our cribbing neighbors to poke into every aspect of our life. At work, the co-workers are always interested in knowing what is going in your life, even if it doesn't concern them. Though some term it as genuine concern, but then again there should be a line which the people should not cross when interacting with others around them.

INTRODUCTION

Prof. Westin maintains that man's need for privacy is rooted in his animal origins and that man and animals share basic mechanisms for claiming privacy among their fellows.[2]

Privacy in the words of **Spencer**[3] "is the continuous adjustment of internal relations to external relations". Adjustment means that in some way an organism related its inner and overt behavior to the requirements of the surroundings. It does not necessarily mean mechanical or scientific adjustments; it means the adjustment that a human is required to make in order to make his behavior socially acceptable for the society and for others around him.

Though many have argued that privacy is more of an interest and not a right and can be invaded for social good, I however have an opposite stance. Privacy is an absolute right, yet it has its limitations to the extent that this right doesn't allow us to mess up someone's personal space. This right is absolute to the extent that the person to him it is conferred should be able to enjoy the right without any alien interference, by alien I mean unauthorized interference.

---

[2]   Alan F. Westin, Privacy and Freedom, 8.

[3]   Spencer, Principles of Biology, Intro. 99

While critics have argued that privacy laws in India are notoriously weak because of the absence of a comprehensive legislation, the reality is somewhat different. I would argue that this unquestioned assumption is based on a paradigm that does not take into consideration that the conception of privacy in India is quite different from the Western conception of the same right.

Firstly, the Indian perception of the word 'privacy' refers to privacy in terms of personal space and subjects. Secondly, even in the West it is not clear what is protected, what is believed to be protected, what is actually protected and what is not protected in terms of privacy. In the course of this book, I will further argue that one's private sphere is subjective and depends on one's culture, environment and economic condition.

Social patterns and values today are too diverse, decentralized, and purposefully dissimilar to provide a foundation for general rules of discourse at the level of specificity required for the protection of privacy. This does not imply that a legal concept of privacy should be disregarded; instead, protection can be defined as specifically or as generally as the legislature chooses by taking into consideration the cultural context and allow its contours to fit within the social and economic conditions. It is important that we explore these foundations for the purposes of identifying the assumptions, assessing its justifications, and analyzing the paradoxical effects of India's privacy policies.

It is 30 years since a Congress Member of Parliament, V.N. Gadgil, suggested an Act for the protection of privacy, designed, no doubt, to curb press exposure of the wrongdoings of politicians. In reality, it is all but impossible to draft a statute that strikes a fair balance between people's right to know and the protection of a person's privacy. In India, as in the United Kingdom, there is no tort of privacy. India's law of torts (that is, civil wrongs punishable in damages) is based on case law, English and foreign. However, the Supreme Court of India has inferred right to privacy from the ones explicitly guaranteed. Article 21 of the Constitution contains a guarantee of personal liberty and it is obvious that personal liberty also involves the right to privacy.

One of the most important ingredients of Article 21 is the expression 'Personal Liberty'. This expression is of the widest amplitude and it includes various kinds of rights like. Right to locomotion, Right to travel abroad, Right of a prisoner to speedy trial

To the same effect are the following observations of **Webster**: "Liberty is the creation of law, essentially different from the authorized licentiousness that trespasses on right, it is a legal and refined idea, the offspring of high civilization, which the savage never understand, and never can understand. Liberty exists in proportion to wholesome restraint; the more restraint on others to keep-off from us, the more liberty we have. It is an error to suppose that liberty consists in a paucity of laws. The working of our complex system, full of checks and restraints on legislative, executive and judicial power is favourable to liberty and justice. These checks arid restraints are so many safeguards set around individual rights and interests. That man is free who is protected from injury"

PRIVACY & THE RIGHT TO PRIVACY DEFINED

"If I were a dictator, religion and state would be separate. I swear by my religion. I will die for it. But it is my personal affair. The state has nothing to do with it. The state would look after your secular welfare, health, communications, foreign relations, currency and so on, but not your or my religion. That is everybody's personal concern!" – **Mahatma Gandhi**

The above words quoted from a speech given by Mahatma Gandhi clearly lay down the definition of privacy or I should say personal liberty in the Indian context. The state should be concerned about fiscal and other aspects of a citizen and not what he does every single day, who he worships, how he worships, what does he wear, what does he eat etc. such aspects of life on an individual is not what the state shall be concerned about.

For some, privacy is a psychological state, a condition of "being-apart-from others" closely related to alienation. For others, privacy is a form of power, "the control we have over information about ourselves", or the condition under which there is control over acquaintance with one's personal affairs by the one's enjoying it.

The **Black's Law Dictionary** defines the right to privacy as, "right to be let alone; the right of a person to be free from unwarranted publicity; and the right to live without unwarranted interference by the public in matters with which the public is not necessarily concerned".

The quest of privacy is an inherent instant of all human beings. As a matter of fact it is a natural need of an individual to establish individual boundaries with almost perfect seclusion. The concept of privacy in its broad sweep covers a number of prospects like nondisclosure of information, sexual affairs, business secrets and nonobservance by others. It may be said that the privacy is antithesis of being public, if any private letters to one's fiend are published by anyone without his express or implied permission then his privacy would come to be violated. Similarly if one's neighbor peeps into in his house from outside then it would also constitute violation of his right to privacy. Thus privacy is a state of isolation and separation from others.

According to Prof. Westin[4], the functions of privacy in democratic societies can be grouped under following four headings:

(a) Personal Autonomy;

(b) Emotional Release;

(c) Self-Evaluation;

(d) Limited and Protected Communication.

---

[4] Alan F. Westin, Privacy and freedom, 32

• **Personal Autonomy**

This most serious threat to the individual's autonomy is the possibility that someone may penetrate the inner zone and learn his ultimate secrets, either by physical or psychological means. The deliberate penetration of individual's protective shell, his psychological armor, would leave him naked to ridicule and shame and would put him under the control of those who knew his secrets. The autonomy that privacy protects is also vital to the development of individuality and consciousness of individual choice in life. This development of individuality is particularly important in democratic societies since qualities of independents thought, diversity of views and non-conformity are considered desirable traits of individuals.

Privacy is a special kind of independence, which can be understood as an attempt to secure autonomy in at least a few personal and spiritual concerns, if necessary in defiance of all the pressures of modern society... It seeks to erect an unreachable wall of dignity and reserve against the entire world. The free man is the private man, the man who still keeps some of his thoughts and judgments entirely to himself, who feel no over-riding compulsion to share everything of value with others, not even those he loves and trusts.

- **<u>Emotional Release:</u>**

Social scientist agrees that each person constantly plays a series of varied and multiple roles depending on his audience and behavioral situation.[5]

On any given day a man may move through the roles of stern father, loving husband, car-pool comedian, skilled lathe operator, union steward, water-cooler flirt and American legion committee chairman all psychologically different roles that he adopts as he moves from scene to scene on the social stage.

Some norms are formally adopted perhaps as law which society really expects many persons to break. This ambivalence produces a situation in which almost everyone does break some social or institutional norms for example, violating traffic laws, breaking sexual mores, cheating on expenses accounts, overstating income tax deductions or smoking in rest rooms when this is prohibited.

Yet another aspect of release is the "safety- valve" function afforded by privacy Most need to give vent to their anger at "the system", "City- hall", "the boss", and various others who exercise authority over them, and to do this in the intimacy of family or friendship circles or in private papers, without fear of being held responsible for such comments. This is very different from freedom of speech or press, which involves publicly voiced criticism without fear of interference by government and subject only to private suit.

---

[5]   Goffman, "Presentation of Self" quoted by Alan F. Westin, Privacy and freedom,34

- **Self- Evaluation**

Every individual needs to integrate his experiences into a meaningful pattern and to exert his individually on events. To carry on such self- evaluation, privacy is essential. This is particularly true of creative persons. Studies of creativity show that it is in reflective solitude and even "day dreaming" during moments of reserve that most creative "non – verbal thoughts takes place. At such moments the individual runs ideas and impressions through his mind in a flow of associations; the active presence of others tends to inhibit this process.

The evaluative function of privacy also has a major moral dimension – the exercise of conscience by which the individual "repossesses himself". While people often consider the moral consequences of their acts during the course of daily affairs, it is primarily in period of privacy that they take a moral inventory of ongoing conduct and measure current performance against personal ideals.

Thus, periods for rumination over past events and for communication with oneself have been said to be "institutionalized in all societies".

A final contribution of privacy to evaluation is its role in the proper timing of the decision to move from private reflection or intimate conversation to a more general publication of acts and thoughts. This is the process by which one tests his own evaluations against the responses of his peers.

- **Limited and Protected Communication**

The greatest threat to civilized social life would be a situation in which each individual was utterly candid in his communications with others, saying exactly what he knew or felt at all times. The havoc done to interpersonal relations by children, saints, mental patients and adult "innocents" is legendary.

Privacy for limited and protected communication has two general aspects. First, it provides the individual with the opportunity he needs for sharing confidences and intimacies with that he trusts-spouse, "the family", personal friends and close associates at work. The individual discloses because he knows that breach of confidence violates social norms in a civilized society.

To protect freedom of limited communication, such relationships – with doctors, lawyers, ministers, psychiatrists and others – are given varying but important degrees of legal privilege against forced disclosure. The privilege given to the religious confessional in domestic societies is well known, but the need for confession is so general that those without religious commitment have institutionalized their substitutes in psychiatric and counseling services.

In its second general aspect, privacy through limited communication serves to set necessary boundaries of mental distance in interpersonal situations ranging from the most intimate to the most formal and public. In marriage, for example, husbands and wives need to retain islands of privacy in the midst of their intimacy if they are to preserve a saving respect and mystery in the relation. These elements of reserved communication will range from small matters, involving management of money, personal habits and outside activities, to the more serious levels of past experiences and inner secrets of personality.

Having discussed the above specific functions of privacy, Prof. Westin further observes that privacy functions basically as an instrument for achieving individual goals of self-realization. As such, it is only part of the individual's complex and shifting system of social needs, part of the way he adjusts his emotional mechanism to the barrage of personal and social stimuli that he encounters in daily life. Individuals have needs for disclosure and companionship every bit as important as their need for privacy. To be left in privacy when one wants to have companionship is as uncomfortable as the inability to have privacy when one craves it. This balance of privacy and disclosure will be powerfully influenced, of course, by both the society's cultural norms and the particular individual's status and life situation.

In the light of such a brilliant and detailed description of the functions of privacy as Prof. Westin has mentioned above, it seems rather difficult to add anything more to it. However, his entire description is predicated upon a free democratic and civilized social life.

The functional justification of privacy as a human right lies in protecting human beings against emotional disturbances of anxiety, humiliation, embarrassment, disgrace, inconvenience annoyance, shame and feeling of indignity. It protects morals and ideas of decency. In view of the above judicial pronouncements, the right to privacy can be availed of by natural persons only and that a corporation or a partnership cannot claim it. It is a personal right which dies with the individual. The right is not assignable as well.

"Privacy is the right to be left alone." This expression was used by Justice Cooley in 1888. This abbreviated meaning of privacy was followed by Samuel Warren and Lois Brandeis in 1890 in one of their articles.[6] They were of view that object of privacy is to protect 'inviolate personality'. They elaborated the proposition and said that in early times the law gave remedy only for interference with life and property, for trespasses *vi et armis*. Then the right to life served only to protect life from battery in its various forms; later there came recognition of spiritual nature and his feelings and his intellect. Acc to Warren and Brandeis the principle which protects personal writings and all other personal productions, not against theft and physical appropriation, but against publication in any form, is in reality, not the principle of private property, but that of inviolate personality. Acc to them the existing law then afforded the principle which may be invoked to protect the privacy of the individual from invasion either by the too enterprising press, the photographer, or the possessor of any other modern device for recording or reproducing scenes or sounds.

In my opinion the main thrust of Warren and Brandeis article revolves on two points. In the first place, they have advocated the necessity of affording the legal protection of

---

[6]   Samuel D. Warren and Lois Brandeis, "The Right to Privacy," 4 Harvard Law Review, 193 (1980)

privacy and secondly, the courts should grant such protection by extending the application of already existing principles of common law. The interest in privacy, as they have propagated is an interest of personality and not property, therefore the argument that common law principles on property, both intellectual and artistic are instance of general right to privacy, doesn't seem much convincing to me.

Rubenfield defines privacy as "the right to make choices and decisions" which forms "the 'kernel' of autonomy". However, going a step further, he introduces the concept of personhood into the doctrine by stating: "some acts, faculties, or qualities are so important to our identity as persons-as human beings-that they must remain inviolable, at least as against the State.

Richard B. Parker observed that if privacy is defined as a psychological state, it becomes impossible to describe a person who has had his privacy temporarily invaded without his knowledge, since his psychological state is not affected at all by the loss of privacy.

In the words of **Charles Fried**, "privacy is not simply an absence of information about us in the minds of others; rather it is the control we have over information about ourselves...the person who enjoys privacy is able to grant or deny access to others...privacy, thus, is control over knowledge about oneself.[7]

---

[7]   Charles fried, "Privacy", 77 Yale Law Journal (1965) 475, 482-483

Similarly **Arthur R. Miller** defines privacy as the, "individual's ability to control the circulation of information relating to him- a power that often is essential to maintaining social relationship and personal freedom.

The above definitions of privacy in terms of control over information in my opinion are of a narrow perspective, these authors, with due respect to them, in my own opinion have gone a little overboard with the concept of privacy. If privacy only means to control the flow of information about oneself from being led to others without the choice of the person, whose it is, then such an approach would seem partially incorrect and highly incomplete. Not every loss or gain of control over information about one's own self is a loss or gain of privacy.

Right to privacy can be defined as individual right to safeguard certain personal information from public sharing. The right to privacy is the right to be let alone, in the absence of some "reasonable" public interest in a person's activities, like those of celebrities or participants in newsworthy events. Invasion of the right to privacy can be the basis for a lawsuit for damages against the person or entity violating the right.

The law of privacy is the simple principle of an individual asserting his choice to be left alone and to ensure that no one violates his personal space. The need for privacy and its recognition as a right is a recent phenomenon. It is an outcome of the changing dimensions of the society from a group to an individual.

The term "privacy" has been described as "the rightful claim of the individual to determine the extent to which he wishes to share of himself with others and his control over the time, place and circumstances to communicate with others. It means his right to withdraw or to participate as he sees fit. It also means the individual's right to control dissemination of information about himself; it is his own personal possession"[8] another author defines privacy as a "'zero relationship' between two or more persons in the sense that there is no interaction or communication between them if they so choose"[9].

The concept is used to describe not only rights purely in the private domain between individuals but also constitutional rights against the State. The former definition deals with an extent to which a private citizen which includes the media and the general public is entitled to gather personal information about another individual. The latter is about the extent to which government authorities can intrude into the life of the private citizen to keep a watch over his movements through devices such as telephone-tapping or surveillance.[10]

It is very arduous to spell out the entire ambit of the right to privacy but we can spell out broadly what all comes under right to privacy. Broadly speaking, it implies the right to be left alone and not to be troubled by public disclosure of his/her private life without any cogent reason.

---

[8]   Adam Carlyle Breckenridge: The Right to Privacy, 1971.

[9]   Edward Shils, "Privacy: Its Constitution and Vicissitudes", Law and Contemporary Problems 31, No. 2 (Spring 1966).

[10] The Right to Privacy in the Age of Information and Communications by Madhavi Divan : (2002) 4 SCC (Jour) 12

It is one of the most cherished right which every individual possesses as a birth right and which every government must respect to the hilt under all circumstances but sadly and mostly this has not been the case.

Now I shall move on to the next chapter, which deals with the evolution of concept of privacy, the evolution of the right to privacy and the need.

EVOLUTION OF THE CONCEPT

The concept of privacy dates back to the times of our two Indian epics viz. - The Mahabharata and The Ramayana. **Kautilya in his Arthshastra** had laid down a detailed procedure for consulting ministers so as to ward off the possibility of leakage or divulgence of the state policies in the statecraft (legacy of which may be found surviving in the provisions of the colonial legislation, The Indian Official Secrets Act, 1923, even today.) though Kautilya did not deal with the issue of individual privacy, however he laid down the foundations for secrecy to be maintained by the state, which later on gave rise to the concept of individual privacy at the behest of invasion by the state in the life of the individual.

No study as such gives a clear picture as to the existence of detailed concept of right to privacy in ancient India, however a close look at the lifestyle of the ancient man, the duties imposed on them and the approach to inter-personal relationships, reveals the rules respecting one's privacy which also cover the aspects laid down by Prof. Westin, discussed earlier.

Words like 'Ekant' (solitude); 'Raha' (Path/way); 'Gupta' (Secret) and words of similar meaning depict that the concept of privacy was not an alien one for the ancient

Indian Society. The early Indian mythology has this concept which states that disturbing a sage was considered the biggest wrong; therefore people did have a sense of respect towards the right to privacy of the meditating sage.

In the great Indian epic, Ramayana, the rule that a women ought not to be seen by a male stranger seems to be well established in the society described in Ramayana, which is still prevalent in the rural areas of Rajasthan, Haryana and others, though this concept of Ramayana in my opinion doesn't deal with one's right to privacy as such. This is more on the lines of suppression of women. This promotes inequality; well we are not on that. Coming back to Indian mythology, I will now discuss one famous portion from Mahabharata. Draupadi was the common wife of all five pandavas, and to avoid embarrassment to draupadi, a rule was made, which stated that if any one of the five brothers was with draupadi and other sees draupadi when she is in the company of the former, the latter would have to undergo the punishment of banishment for twelve years in the forest. Arjun, once entered the room, when Draupadi was in company of Yudhistra, Arjun had to undergo the punishment of exile. This notion laid down by Mahabharata, does make sense as to the concept of privacy in ancient India to me. People during this time respected each other's right of privacy; they had a sense of right or wrong.

I would like to quote words of a Supreme Court Judge from US Supreme court, here, which talks about the importance of privacy in man's life, when he is executing intimate functions. *"The right of an individual to conduct intimate relationships in the intimacy of his or her own home seems to me to be the heart of constitution's protection of privacy"*. – **Harry A.Blackmun**

If the above mentioned is followed duly by each and every individual, then half of the litigation over the right to privacy would end there itself, however we shall come back to this later. Right to privacy in my opinion was an inalienable right even back then. Privacy is something which is not conferred on a person; it is rather a prerequisite of any living soul, whether he is an infant or a full grown man.

The concept of privacy is in its incipient stages in India. It is more of a customary right rather than any other format. Custom is one of the highly recognized form of law in our country and thus any right which has a customary origin is followed and regarded as a matter of authority in the society that we live in.

It has been observed that according to the philosophical doctrines of vedic rishis, legality of a custom lies in the fact that a need for the act is felt, i.e. something is required and other substitutions haven't helped.

In 1888, the case of **Gokul Prasad v. Radho**[11] came before the division bench of Allahabad High Court for decision. The plaintiff alleged that the defendant had wrongfully built a new house in such a way that certain eaves of that new house projected over the plaintiff's land and that a verandah and certain doors of the house interfered with the privacy of those portions of the plaintiff's house and premises which were occupied and used by the females

---

[11]   ILR 10 All. (1888) 358

of the plaintiff's family. Accordingly he claimed to have the eaves, in question, and the verandah removed and the doors, complained of, be closed. The female members of the plaintiff's family were paradanashin women. The lower court decreed the plaintiff's claims with costs. On appeal, the district judge reversed the decree of the lower court and dismissed the plaintiff's claims. It is against the decree of the district judge that an appeal was made and this is how the case came before the High Court. The division bench of the High Court formulated the following questions. A primary question must in all cases be:

Does the privacy in fact and substantially exist and has it been and is t in fact enjoyed? If it were found that no privacy substantially exists or is enjoyed, there would be no further question in an ordinary case to decide. If, on the other hand, it were found that privacy did substantially exist and enjoyed, the next question would be: was that privacy substantially or materially interfered by the acts of the defendant done without the consent or acquiescence of the person seeking relief against those acts.[12]

Chief Justice, Sir John Edge, who delivered the judgment along with Justice Mahmood, arrived at the conclusion after examining various authorities that a right of privacy exists and has existed in these provinces by usage or custom and that substantial interference with such a right of privacy, where it exists, if the interference with such a right be without the consent of the owner of the dominant tenement, afford such owner a good cause of

---

[12]   ILR 10 All. (1888) 358 at 385-386

action. In his concurring judgement Justice Mahmood pointed out that under circumstances of life such as they are in these provinces, the custom that invasion of privacy is actionable is far well recognized that Mr. Motilal Nehru, for the respondent, in course of his argument stated that it was wholly unnecessary to remand the case for ascertaining the custom. The appeal was decreed and the lower court judgment was restored.

The case stands for the propositions that an intrusion into one's privacy results in a feeling of disgrace. Chief Justice Edge observes:

> *It cannot be doubted that the male relations of a pardah-nashin woman and the woman herself would consider it a disgrace were her face to be exposed to the gaze of male strangers...*[13]

The case propels yet another proposition that privacy, being related to the life style of the people, is a dynamic concept differing in accordance with the different life-styles of different peoples.

Invasion of privacy as an actionable wrong owes its origin to the conditions of life. In a similar case in front of the Bombay High Court, a division bench in the case of *Manishankar Hargovan v. Trikam Narsi*[14] affirmed the decree of the lower appellate court which ordered the closing up of the newly opened doors and windows which

---

[13]   ILR 10 All. (1888) 358 at 385

[14]   5 Bom. H.C.R. (1876) ACJ 42. (The bench consisted of Tucker and Gibbs, JJ.)

commanded the view of the plaintiff's secluded apartment depriving his privacy on the ground that it constituted a substantial invasion of the privacy hitherto enjoyed by the plaintiff. Referring to a series of decisions and the usage of Guzerat, their lordships observed:

> A series of decisions extending over a long number of years, has settled the question, that in accordance with the usage of *Guzerat*, a man, may not open new doors and windows in his house, or make any new apertures, or enlarge old ones, in a way which shall enable him to overlook those portions of his neighbor's premises which are ordinarily secluded from observation, and in this manner to intrude upon that neighbor's privacy; and that an invasion of privacy is an infraction of a right for which the person injured has remedy at law. The ruling has been founded on the long established usage of the province and, though opposed to the doctrine of the English law, must be upheld and affirmed.[15]

In the light of above two judgments and many in which court took the opposite stance such as the *Keshva Harkha v. ganpat Hira chand case*[16]; **the case of Sreenath Dutta v. Nand Kishore Bose**[17] one thing can be clearly established

---

[15]   5 Bom. H.C.R. (1867) ACJ 42 at 44-45

[16]   Justice Melvill and Justice Kemball; 8 Bom H.C.Rep (1871) ACJ 87

[17]   Referred to in 5 B.L.R. (1870) 676, 14 WR 103; Court declined to give relief to the plaintiff ho built an upper storey to his house, overlooking the inner apartments of defendant, defendant built

that the right to privacy has a customary allowance in the country i.e. privacy and its parts, if not the entire right as it is now in the present state, have a customary backing in the country. Even though the cases did not depict a standard or uniform pattern, the mere stating that privacy is a customary right did not accord any protection to the plaintiff or punishment to the defendant, the element of "substantial and material interference" need to be shown and clearly established. If this element was missing, then the courts usually ruled in the favor of defendant.

Privacy might have a customary backing in the country, but the entire gambit of the right to privacy cannot be said to be a part of customary practice in India. This right back in the 18th and the 19th century was more or less related to the issues of construction of houses and paradanashin women. Man as per the history has been lustful creature and does see the women as an object of pleasure and the picture was no difference back then, therefore the right to privacy to the extent of protecting dignity of women is correctly taken up from customary laws.

The custom of privacy should not be carried to an oppressive length and where there is clear remedy available to plaintiff, he should not have anything except by way of damages at the utmost. Though in my opinion, monetary compensation alone is not the correct solution to invasion of privacy, as '*money cannot restore lost dignity*'.

---

a wall to which obstructed the view. The bench stated that no relief to be granted as the plaintiff id the wrong doer.

One question which still remains unanswered as I conclude this chapter to the extent of customary rights is that, if we follow the customary practice, then whether is it correct to state, that the right to privacy was only accorded to occupants of a piece of land or owners alone and not any other simple dwelling soul?

In my opinion, though the customs did talk about privacy and the corresponding right, still the laws did not talk about individual's right to privacy which is one important aspect that I will deal with in this book.

Importance of privacy as a human right and its need for legal protection has been acknowledged in the following three international documents:

1. Article 12 of the Universal Declaration of Human Rights adopted by the General Assembly of the United Nations on December 10, 1948, reads as under:

   No one shall be subjected to arbitrary interference with his privacy, family, home or correspondence, or to attacks upon his honor and reputation. Everyone has the right to the protection of the law against such interference or attacks.

2. Article 17 of the International Covenant on Civil and Political Rights provides as under:

   No one shall be subjected to arbitrary or unlawful interference with his privacy, family, home or correspondence, nor to unlawful attacks on his honor and reputation.

3. Similarly, <u>Article 8 of the European Convention for the protection of Human Rights and fundamental freedoms, 1950</u>, provides that:

    a. Everyone has the right to respect for his private and family life, his home and his correspondence;

    b. There shall be no interference by a public authority with the exercise of this right except such as is in accordance with the law and is necessary in a democratic society in the interests of national security, public safety or the economic well being of the country, for the prevention of disorder or crime for the protection of the rights and freedoms of others.

A number of international conferences[18] have been held emphasizing the need to protect privacy by law. In several countries, legal measures have been adopted to protect the right to privacy, and in many others, committees were appointed to investigate the problems connected with privacy and make suitable recommendations'.

India, it has been said[19], is far behind both Britain and the United States of America in active judicial enforcement or even public discussions of Privacy laws. The lack of demands of public debate on the threat to the right to

---

[18]   22-23 May, 1967, StockHolm, Organised by the Swedish section of the International "Commission of Jurists"; 30 September- 3 October 1970, Brussels, France and Switzerland

[19]   Richard P. Claude (ed). Comparitive Human Rights, P 150

privacy may mislead a casual observer to believe that there are no laws safeguarding this human right in India.[20]

In fact, it has not misled a casual observer only but also jurists, journalist and public man[21] to believe that there is no right to privacy in the Indian legal system. Justice Jagannadhadas has maintained that the Indian constitution does not recognize a fundamental right to privacy and there is no justification to import it by some process of strained construction.[22]

Professor Upendra baxi has taken an extreme stand in subscribing to the view that privacy is alliance to Indian culture. The main reason which gave rise to such climate of opinion is the lack of any serious research in the Indian law on the subject, in question.

It is to dispel such erroneous climate of opinion and as an effort to clean a few layers of dust thus far accumulated on the vaults of law libraries, the present study undertakes a critical examination of the Indian legal system to highlight the safeguards it provides to the right to privacy.

A couple of years prior to the publication of the celebrated article "The Right to Privacy" in the Harvard Law Review[23], in 1888, Chief Justice Edge of the Allahabad High Court observed as follows:

---

[20]   V.R.Krishna Iyer, Justice and Beyond, P 180

[21]   V.N.Gadgil introduced "The Right to Privacy Bill" in Lok Sabha, March 1981

[22]   M.P.Sharma v. Satish Chandra, AIR 1954 SC 300 at 306-307

[23]   4 Har. L. Rev (1890) P. 193

> *In my opinion, the fact that there is no much custom of privacy known to the law of England can have no bearing on the question whether there can be in India an usage or custom of privacy valid in law. The condition of domestic life in the two countries have from remote times been essentially different and in my opinion, it is owing to that difference in the conditions of domestic life alone that a custom which appears to me to be a perfectly reasonable one in India should be unknown in England.*[24]

Urging the right to privacy for the British nationals on the basis of the Indian cases, Percy H. Winfield, in 1931, made an appeal to the House of Commons, wherein he observed:

> *The Indian cases have been referred to not, of course, for the purpose of urging their application to the different particular circumstances which prevail in England, but as an illustration of the pliability of Indian law where the need of protecting privacy has been felt. It will be seen when we pass to consider personal privacy that our law probably lags behind the needs of a community in which intrusion on privacy is apt to take offensive forms owing to the modern development of instantaneous photography and of method of advertisement which to say the least of them, are totally indifferent to the feelings of private individuals.*[25]

---

[24] Golak Prasad v. Radho, ILR 10 All. 358 at 388

[25] 47 Law Quarterly review (1931) P 29-30

CONSTITUTIONAL ASPECTS- INDIA, UNITED STATES & UNITED KINGDOM

When the Constitution was being framed, the word used in the draft Constitution as prepared even up to the stage of Advisory Committee was "liberty" without being qualified the word "liberty" by "personal" being of the view that otherwise "liberty" might be construed very widely so as to include freedoms already dealt under article 19. The result is that article 21 as it finally found place in our Constitution protects "personal liberty[26].

Although the Indian Constitution does not contain an explicit reference to a Right to Privacy, this right has been read in to the constitution by the Supreme Court as a component of two Fundamental Rights: the right to freedom under Article 19 and the right to life and personal liberty under Article 21.

It would be instructive to provide a brief background to each of these Articles before delving deeper into the privacy jurisprudence expounded by the courts under them. Part III of the Constitution of India (Articles 12 through 35) is titled 'Fundamental Rights' and lists out several rights

---

[26] KailashRai "Constitutional Law of India", Central Law Publications, (2001)pg 170

which are regarded as fundamental to all citizens of India (some fundamental rights, notably the right to life and liberty apply all persons in India, whether they are 'citizens' or not). Article 13 forbids the State from making "any law which takes away or abridges" the fundamental rights.

Article 19(1)(a) stipulates that "All citizens shall have the right to freedom of speech and expression". However this is qualified by Article 19(2) which states that this will not "affect the operation of any existing law, or prevent the State from making any law, in so far as such law imposes reasonable restrictions on the exercise of the right ... in the interests of the sovereignty and integrity of India, the security of the State, friendly relations with foreign States, public order, decency or morality, or in relation to contempt of court, defamation or incitement to an offence".

Thus the Freedom of Expression guaranteed by Article 19(1)(a) is not absolute, but a qualified right that is susceptible, under the Constitutional scheme, to being curtailed under specified conditions.

The other important Fundamental Right from the perspective of privacy jurisprudence is Article 21 which reads:

> "No person shall be deprived of his life or personal liberty except according to procedure established by law."

Though the terminology of the abovementioned article starts with an expression of deprivation, the fundamental aim of Article 21 is to prevent impingement upon personal liberty, space and air and deprivation of life except according to procedure established by the law of the land. It certainly implies that this fundamental right has been provided against the state only. If an act of private individual amounts to encroachment upon the personal liberty or deprivation of life of other person, such violation would not fall under the parameters set for article 21. In such a case the remedy for aggrieved person would be either under Article 226 of the constitution or under general law. But, where an act of private individual supported by the state infringes the personal liberty or life of another person, the act will certainly come under the ambit of Article 21, article 21 of the Constitution deals with prevention of encroachment upon personal liberty or deprivation of life of a person.[27]

The state cannot be defined in a restricted sense. It includes Government Departments, Legislature, Administration, Local Authorities exercising statutory powers and so on so forth, but it does not include non-statutory or private bodies having no statutory powers. For example: company, autonomous body and others. Therefore, the fundamental right guaranteed under Article 21 relates only to the acts of State or acts under the authority of the State which is not according to procedure established by law. The main object of Article 21 is that before a person is deprived of his life or personal liberty by the State, the procedure established by law must be strictly followed. Right to Life means the right to lead meaningful, complete and dignified life. It does not have restricted meaning. It is something more than surviving or animal existence. The

---

[27]   (2002) 4 SCC (Jour) 12

meaning of the word life cannot be narrowed down and it will be available not only to every citizen of the country. As far as Personal Liberty is concerned, it means freedom from physical restraint of the person by personal incarceration or otherwise and it includes all the varieties of rights other than those provided under Article 19 of the Constitution. Procedure established by Law means the law enacted by the State. Deprived has also wide range of meaning under the Constitution. These ingredients are the soul of this provision. The fundamental right under Article 21 is one of the most important rights provided under the Constitution which has been described as heart of fundamental rights by the Apex Court.

The right to freedom of speech and expression and the right to privacy are two sides of the same coin. One person's right to know and be informed may violate another's right to be left alone. Just as the freedom of speech and expression is vital for the dissemination of information on matters of public interest, it is equally important to safeguard the private life of an individual to the extent that it is unrelated to public duties or matters of public interest. The law of privacy endeavors to balance these competing freedoms.

The very first case to lay down the contours of the right to privacy in India, was the case of ***Kharak Singh* v. *State of Uttar Pradesh***[28] where a Supreme Court bench of seven judges was required to decide the constitutionality of certain police regulations which allowed the police to conduct domiciliary visits and surveillance of persons with

---

[28]   (1964) SCR (1) 332,

a criminal record. The petitioner in this case had challenged the constitutionality of these regulations on the grounds that they violated his fundamental right to privacy under the 'personal liberty' clause of Article 21 of the Constitution. In this case a majority of the judges refused to interpret Article 21 to include within its ambit the right to privacy part the majority stated "The right of privacy is not a guaranteed right under our Constitution, and therefore the attempt to ascertain the movements of an individual is merely a manner in which privacy is invaded and is not an infringement of a fundamental right guaranteed in Part III." The majority however did recognize the common law right of citizens to enjoy the liberty of their houses and approved of the age old saying that a man's home was his castle. The majority therefore understood the term 'personal liberty' in Article 21 in the context of age old principles from common law while holding domiciliary visits to be unconstitutional. Two of the judges of the seven judge bench, however, saw the right to privacy as a part of Article 21, marking an early recognition of privacy as a fundamental right. Justice Subba Rao held "It is true our Constitution does not expressly declare a right to privacy as a fundamental right, but the said right is an essential ingredient of personal liberty."

The question of privacy as a fundamental right presented itself once again to the Supreme Court a few years later in the case of ***Govind v. State of Madhya Pradesh***[29] The petitioner in this case had challenged, as unconstitutional, certain police regulations on the grounds that the regulations violated his fundamental right to privacy. Although the

---

[29] (AIR 1975 SC 1378)

issues were similar to the *Kharak Singh* case, the three judges hearing this particular case were more inclined to grant the right to privacy the status of a fundamental right. Justice Mathew stated:

> "Rights and freedoms of citizens are set forth in the Constitution in order to guarantee that the individual, his personality and those things stamped with his personality shall be free from official interference except where a reasonable basis for intrusion exists. 'Liberty against government' a phrase coined by Professor Corwin expresses this idea forcefully. In this sense, many of the fundamental rights of citizens can be described as contributing to the right to privacy."

Balancing the 'right to privacy' against the 'right to free speech'

The Supreme Court balanced the right of privacy against the right to free speech in the case of ***R. Rajagopal v. State of Tamil Nadu***[30]. In this case, the petitioner was a Tamil newsmagazine which had sought directions from the Court to restrain the respondent State of Tamil Nadu and its officers to not interfere in the publication of the autobiography of a death row convict–'Auto Shankar' which contained details about the nexus between criminals and police officers. The Supreme Court framed the questions in these terms: "Whether a citizen of this country can prevent

---

[30]   (1994 SCC (6) 632)

another person from writing his life story or biography? Does such unauthorized writing infringe the citizen's right to privacy? Whether the freedom of press guaranteed by Article 19(1) (a) entitles the press to publish such unauthorized account of a citizen's life and activities? If so then to what extent and in what circumstances?"

While answering the above questions, a bench of two judges of the Supreme Court, for the first time, directly linked the right to privacy to Article 21 of the Constitution but at the same time excluded matters of public record from being protected under this 'Right to Privacy'. The Supreme Court held:

> "(1) the right to privacy is implicit in the right to life and liberty guaranteed to the citizens of this country by Article 21. It is a "right to be let alone". A citizen has a right to safeguard the privacy of his own, his family, marriage, procreation, motherhood, child-bearing and education among other matters. None can publish anything concerning the above matters without his consent whether truthful or otherwise and whether laudatory or critical. If he does so, he would be violating the right to privacy of the person concerned and would be liable in an action for damages. Position may, however, be different, if a person voluntarily thrusts himself into controversy or voluntarily invites or raises a controversy. (2) The rule aforesaid is subject to the exception, that any publication concerning the aforesaid aspects becomes unobjectionable if such publication is based upon public records including court records.

This is for the reason that once a matter becomes a matter of public record, the right to privacy no longer subsists and it becomes a legitimate subject for comment by press and media among others."

In the light of decisions of the Hon'ble Supreme Court, the word 'Live' and 'Liberty' are liberally interpreted. Article 21 is now being invoked almost as a residuary right. Expansion of Article 21 has led to many of the directive principles (which are not justiciable) being enforced as fundamental rights. On account of this expanded interpretation, now the right to pollution free water and air, right to food clothing, environment, protection of cultural heritage, Right to every child to a full development, Right of persons residing in hilly areas to have access to roads and Right to education (**Mohini Jain v. State of Karnataka**[31]) have all found their way into Article 21.

One other remarkable feature of the expanded meaning given to Article 21 is that though it is in the form of a negative duty cast upon the State not to interfere with life and liberty of individual, yet various decisions of the Hon'ble Supreme Court have now imposed positive obligations on the State to take various steps for ensuring enjoyment of life by an individual with dignity.

Thus every condition, i.e., conducive for leading a better life with human dignity is brought within the fold of Article 21. The State is now enjoined to fulfil these positive obligations.

---

[31]   AIR 1992 SC 1858

For eg. Maintenance and employment of public health, elimination of pollution, improvement of means of communication, rehabilitation of bonded labourers, providing human conditions in prisons and protective homes, all come under Article 21 of the Constitution

Position in the U.S. and the U.K.

Even in the United States and Britain, legal recognition to privacy came in slow stages. It began with an article in 1890 in the Harvard Law Review by Louis D. Brandeis and his friend and law partner, Samuel Warren. Entitled "The Right to Privacy", it was widely noticed. In 1928, as a judge of the Supreme Court, Brandeis gave a vigorous dissent upholding this right, which he called "the right to be let alone". This was in Olmstead vs U.S., the famous telephone tapping case. The majority ruled that evidence, thus obtained, was admissible in courts. The ruling has suffered much battering since.

English common law recognized no right to privacy. Committees were set up to consider legislation on the right to privacy, only to find that no easy solution was possible. Reconciliation of this right with the freedom of speech is not an easy task. However, the Human Rights Act, 1998, "incorporates" as British law the "European Convention for the Protection of Human Rights and Fundamental Freedoms" signed in 1950. Article 8(1) of the Convention says that "everyone has the right to respect for his private and family life, his home and his correspondence". Clause (2) carves out permissible restrictions, which are "necessary in a democratic society" in the interests of national security, for the prevention of crime, etc. Several cases have since been decided in English courts, which are of direct relevance to us.

The **American law on privacy**[32] has evolved faster than the law in England.[33] One of the earliest cases in England, ***Albert* v. *Strange***[34] involved the unauthorized copying of etchings made by Queen Victoria and her husband for their private amusement. The etchings, which represented members of the Royal family and matters of personal interest, were entrusted to a printer for making impressions. An employee of the printer made unauthorized copies and sold them to the defendant who in turn proposed to exhibit them publicly. Prince Albert succeeded in obtaining an injunction to prevent the exhibition. The court's reasoning was based on both the enforcement of the Prince's property rights as well as the employee's breach of confidence. This case is widely regarded as having inspired the development of the law of privacy in the United States.

Even as late as 1991, the law in England was found to be inadequate in protecting privacy. In that year, the Court of appeal decided ***Kaye* v. *Robertson.***[35] The case concerned a well-known actor who had to be hospitalized after sustaining

---

[32]   (2002) 4 SCC (Jour) 12

[33]   Ironically, it was by borrowing from the English case-law and creatively interpreting it that the law in America developed. And yet, the law of privacy in England has lagged far behind, inviting serious criticism from commentators.

[34]   (1849) 1 Mac & G 25 : 41 ER 1171

[35]   (1991) FSR 62

serious head injuries in a car accident. At a time when the actor was in no condition to be interviewed, a reporter and a photographer from the *Sunday Sport* newspaper gained unauthorized access to his hospital room, took photographs and attempted to conduct an interview with the actor. An interlocutory injunction was sought on behalf of the actor to prevent the paper from publishing the article which claimed that Kaye had agreed to give an exclusive interview to the paper. There being no right to privacy under the English law, the plaintiff could not maintain an action for breach of privacy. In the absence of such a right, the claim was based on other rights of action such as libel, malicious falsehood and trespass to the person, in the hope that one or the other would help him protect his privacy. Eventually, he was granted an injunction to restrain publication of the malicious falsehood. The publication of the story and some less objectionable photographs were, however, allowed on the condition that it was not claimed that the plaintiff had given his consent. The remedy was clearly inadequate since it failed to protect the plaintiff from preserving his personal space and from keeping his personal circumstances away from public glare. The court expressed its inability to protect the privacy of the individual and blamed the failure of common law and statute to protect this right.[36]

In the U.S.A., the need for a law to protect privacy was articulated as early as 1890 when an article titled "The

---

[36] Hopefully, the Human Rights Act in 1998 which imposes a positive obligation to act in accordance with the European Convention on Human Rights will have a positive effect on the development of the law in the U.K.

Right to Privacy" was published by Warren and Brandeis[37] This article laid the intellectual foundations for the law on privacy.

"Recent inventions and business method call attention to the next step which must be taken for the protection of the person, and for securing to the individual what Judge Cooley calls 'the right to be let alone'. Instantaneous photographs and newspaper enterprise have invaded the sacred precincts of the home... private devices threaten to make good the prediction that 'what is whispered in the closet shall be proclaimed from the house tops'... The press is overstepping in every direction the obvious bounds of propriety and of decency. Gossip is no longer the resource of the idle and of the vicious, but has become a trade, which is pursued with industry as well as effrontery... The intensity and complexity of life attendant upon advancing civilization, have rendered necessary some retreat from the world, and man, under the refining influence of culture, has become more sensitive to publicity, so that solitude and privacy have become more essential to the individual; but modern enterprise and invention have through invasions upon his privacy, subjected him to mental pain and distress, far greater than could be inflicted by bodily injury. It is our purpose to consider whether the existing law affords a principle which can properly be invoked to protect the privacy of an individual; and, if it does, what the nature and extent of such protection is..."

---

[37]   4 Harvard Law Rev. 193

The most well-known American cases on privacy are ***Griswold v. Connecticut***[38] and ***Roe v. Wade***[39]. In *Griswold* the constitutionality of a law which prohibited the use of contraceptives was challenged. Upholding the notion of privacy, Justice Douglas held:

> "...'Governmental purpose to control or prevent activities constitutionally subject to State regulation may not be achieved by means which sweep unnecessarily broadly and thereby invade the area of protected freedoms'. (***NAACP v. Alabama***[40]) Would we allow the police to search the sacred precincts of marital bedrooms for telltale signs of the use of contraceptives? The very idea is repulsive to the notions of privacy surrounding the marriage relationship."[41]

Striking down the legislation as an unconstitutional invasion of the right to marital privacy, it was held that the right of freedom of speech and the press includes not only the right to utter or to print but also to distribute, receive and read and that without those peripheral rights, the specific right would be endangered.

Roe* v. *Wade dealt with the right of an unmarried pregnant woman to an abortion. Upholding the woman's right to make that choice which affected her private life,

---

[38]   381 US 479 (1965)

[39]   410 US 113 (1973)

[40]   377 US 288, 307 (1964)

[41]   381 US 479, 486 (1965)

the Supreme Court held that although the American Constitution did not explicitly mention any right of privacy, the Supreme Court itself recognized such a right as a guarantee of certain "zones or areas of privacy" and "that the roots of that right may be found in the First Amendment, in the Fourth and Fifth Amendments, in the penumbras of the Bill of Rights and in the concept of liberty guaranteed by the Fourteenth Amendment".

In **Doe v. Borough of Barrington**[42] the court held that a police officer violated constitutional right of privacy by disclosing that a person was infected with HIV. The facts of this case are as follows:

> Jane Doe, her husband and friend, were traveling in the plaintiff's truck when police officer of Borough of Barrington stopped the truck and questioned the occupants. Police officer arrested them and then releases Jane Doe and her friend from custody but detained Jane Doe's husband on charges of unlawful possession of hypodermic needle. When he was initially arrested, Jane Doe's husband told the police officer that he had tested HIV positive and therefore officers should be careful in searching him.

> Later on the same day Jane Doe and her friend drove her friend's car to the Doe residence. The car engine was left running, and the car apparently slipped into gear, rolling down the driveway into a neighbor's fence. Two police officers from

---

[42] , 729 F.Supp. 376 (D.N.J.,1990)

Runnemede, the area where later incident happen, Steven Van Camp and one of the defendants Russell Smith, responded to the radio call about the incident. While they were at the scene, Detective Preen of the Barrington police arrived and, in a private conversation with Van Camp, revealed that Jane Doe's husband had been arrested earlier in the day and had told Barrington police officers that he had AIDS. Van Camp then told defendant Smith.

After Jane Doe and her friend left the immediate vicinity, defendant Smith told the defendant neighbor that Jane Doe's husband had AIDS and that, to protect herself, she should wash with disinfectant. Defendant became upset upon hearing this information. Neighbor's wife, one of the defendants was employee in the school where children of plaintiff were studying. Knowing that the four Doe children attending the Downing School in Runnemede, the same school that her own daughter attending, defendant neighbor contacted other parents with children in the school. She also contacted the media. The next day, eleven parents removed nineteen children from the Downing School due to a panic over the Doe children's attending the school. The media was present, and the story was covered in the local newspapers and on television. At least one of the reports mentioned the name of the Doe family. Plaintiffs allege that as a result of the disclosure, they have suffered harassment, discrimination, and humiliation. They allege they have been shunned by the community.

Plaintiffs brought this civil rights action against the police officer Smith and the municipalities of Barrington and Runnemede for violations of their federal constitutional rights pursuant to 42 U.S.C. 1983 (1982) (Civil action for deprivation of rights). The federal constitutional right is their right to privacy under the fourteenth amendment. The suit contains pendent state claims against defendant neighbor for invasion of privacy and intentional infliction of emotional distress.

The court upholding privacy right finds that the constitution protects plaintiffs from government disclosure of their husband's infection with the AIDS virus. The court cited United States Supreme Court decision in **Whalen v. Roe,**[43] stating the Court has recognized that the fourteenth amendment protects two types of privacy interest? One is the individual interest in avoiding disclosure of personal matters, and another is the interest in independence in making certain kinds of important decisions? The court said that disclosure of a family member's medical condition, especially exposure to or infection with the AIDS virus is a disclosure of a personal matter.

The court finds that defendants police officer Smith and district administration of Runnemede violated plaintiff's constitutional right to privacy and administration's failure to train their official

---

[43]   429 U.S. 589, 599-600 (1977)

about AIDS and that defendants are liable under 42 U.S.C. § 1983 (1982) (Civil action for deprivation of rights).

In **Chizmar v. Mackie**,[44] the Supreme Court of Alaska refused to hold a physician liable for breach of confidentiality after informing a patient's spouse of her condition without her authorization. The facts of this case as follows:

> Savitri Chizmar, a native of Trinidad and Tobago, has lived in the United States since 1980. She was married to Matthew Chizmar. There were two children of this marriage, aged five and seven at the time of the events in question. In February 1989 Savitri was admitted to Providence Hospital, suffering from pneumonia and gastritis. Dr. Scott Mackie was the admitting physician. Upon her admission, Matthew signed the hospital's standard admission consent form on his wife's behalf, because she was "too sick" for the paperwork. This form states that the patient consents to procedures that may be performed during hospitalization, including laboratory procedures.

> While at Providence, Dr. Mackie ordered that a battery of laboratory tests be run on Savitri's blood. As part of this testing, Savitri was tested for HIV/AIDS, using the HIV ELISA screen. Dr. Mackie did not discuss with Savitri the specific tests that were being run and did not inform Savitri that he was testing her for AIDS.

---

[44]   896 P.2d 196 (Alaska 1995)

Savitri's initial HIV ELISA screen was found to be "repeatedly reactive." The report stated that confirmatory tests were being performed and that "[n]o interpretation of the patient's HIV antibody status is possible until the confirmatory assay has been completed." Dr. Mackie believed that this result meant that Savitri had tested positive for the HIV virus. Dr. Mackie felt that it was necessary to advise Savitri of the result quickly.

Initially, however, he did not inform Savitri of his conclusion. Instead, he decided to ask her husband to help break the news to her.

Several days after Matthew and Dr. Mackie informed Savitri of the test result, Dr. Janis, an HIV specialist, examined and interviewed Savitri. Dr. Janis concluded that the test result was most likely a "false positive" and testified that he was confident that he had so informed Savitri. Dr. Mackie testified that, prior to Savitri's discharge, he informed her that the test was probably a "false positive" and that she would need to be retested to make sure.

Savitri left the hospital on the day she was informed of the test result. From that point forward, she and her husband experienced a severe escalation of what had been periodic domestic problems and violence. They fought regularly and, on at least one occasion, Matthew allegedly beat Savitri. The fighting further escalated after Matthew tested negative for HIV.

Three weeks after her discharge, Savitri and her husband reviewed her medical records. Included within these records was the discharge summary, which expressly stated "False positive HIV test." The records also included a notation from Dr. Janis concluding that it was likely that the HIV test was a false positive test. Subsequently, in April, a retest established that Savitri did not have AIDS.

Matthew left the marital home in May 1989 and two months after Savitri received the final test result establishing that she did not have AIDS, he filed for divorce in June. The divorce became final in March 1990. After the divorce, Matthew moved to California.

Savitri, individually and on behalf of her children, filed suit against Dr. Mackie. In her personal action, she alleged that Dr. Mackie did not have Savitri's informed consent to conduct the initial HIV/AIDS test. She also alleged that Dr. Mackie breached his duty of confidentiality owed to Savitri by informing her husband of the test results. The complaint asserted that, as a result of Dr. Mackie's negligence and breach of duty, she suffered damages, including severe emotional distress. Savitri later amended her complaint to encompass Dr. Mackie's allegedly negligent misdiagnosis of AIDS.

In his answer, Dr. Mackie admitted that the initial HIV test was performed without specific consent and that he informed Matthew of the test results. In September 1991, the superior court, Judge Hunt, entered partial summary judgment in favor of Savitri on the issue of Dr. Mackie's breach of the duty of confidentiality. However, the court concluded that questions of fact remained as to whether Dr. Mackie's breach was justified.

The case went to the Supreme Court of Alaska. On the issue of right to privacy the court held that the constitutional right to privacy is a right against government action, not against the actions of private parties. Thus, to the extent her argument is based on the Alaska Constitution, her claim must fail. The court also reasoned that Savitri also fails to present a persuasive argument under common law invasion of privacy principles. There are four branches of the common law right to privacy, as recognized in the Restatement (Second) of Torts Section 652A-E, at 376 (1977). None of these sections can be read to support Savitri's claim in the present case.

Further the court justified its stand by citing a case **MacDonald v. Clinger**, [45] state that Disclosure of confidential information… to a spouse will be justified whenever there is a danger to the patient, the spouse, or another person; otherwise information should not be disclosed without authorization.

---

[45]   446 N.Y.S.2d 801

Justification or excuse will depend upon a showing of circumstances and competing interests which support the need to disclose. The court also relied on a case holding that a doctor, having diagnosed an illness, may be liable for failure to warn patient's family members.

Right to Privacy Under Constitution of India

There are several customary rules prevailing in India which protect the privacy interest of an individual. Similarly constitutional provisions have provided a protective umbrella to this right. Besides customary rules and constitutional provisions several other statutes recognize right to privacy directly or indirectly. The framers of Constitution of India secured an elaborated scheme of protection of individual liberties under the heading of fundamental right, but strange enough it did not included right to privacy. In the Constituent Assembly and amendment on the lines of the Fourth Amendment of the United States Constitution was moved by Kazi Syed Karimuddin and it was also supported by Dr. B. R. Ambedkar. However, Dr, Ambedkar's support was a little reserved one and not forceful enough to secure incorporation of right to privacy in the Constitution. Possibly the Constituent Assembly members did not visualize the importance of the right to privacy as an aspect of personal liberty. Hence, in the succeeding pages the authors have made an endeavour to study the constitutional provisions because any right protected under the Constitution deserves some higher importance. Further, if any right is made as a fundamental right under the document of the land, it becomes sometimes a basic feature of the Constitution. Half a century has passed since India framed its Constitution and still the Indian Constitution does not recognize privacy as an inherent Fundamental Right. Privacy as one of the necessary ingredients of personal liberty suffered heavily because of its non-inclusion. Whereas the Constitution does not mention expressly the right to privacy, Article 21 miraculously has been playing a major role in the safeguard of privacy as an essential ingredient of personal liberty. It is again important to note the Article 21 by itself has not been a potent enough weapon in defence of privacy until it is sharpened and made effective by judicial activism.

In **R. Rajagopal v. State of T.N.**[46] popularly known as "*Auto Shanker* case" the Hon'ble Supreme Court has expressly held the "right to privacy" or the right to be let alone is guaranteed by Art.21 of the Constitution. A citizen has a right to safeguard the privacy of his own, his family, marriage, procreation, motherhood, child-bearing and education among other matters. None can publish anything concerning the above matters without his consent whether truthful or otherwise and whether laudatory or critical. If he does so, he would be violating the right of the person concerned and would be liable in an action for damages. However, position may be differed if he voluntarily puts into controversy or voluntarily invites or raises a controversy.

This rule is subject to an exception that if any publication of such matters is based on public record including court record it will be unobjectionable. If a matter becomes a matter of public record the right to privacy no longer exists

---

[46]   (1994) 6 SCC 632

and it becomes a legitimate subject for comment by press and media among others. Again, an exception must be carved out of this rule in the interests of decency under Art. 19(2) in the following cases, viz, a female who is the victim of a sexual assault, kidnapping, addiction or a like offence should not further be subjected to the indignity of her name and the incident being published in press or media.

The second exception is that the right to privacy or the remedy of action for damage is simply not available to public officials as long as the criticism concerns the discharge of their public duties; not even when the publication is based on untrue facts and statements unless the official can establish that the statement had been made with reckless disregard of truth.

The Court, however, held that the judiciary with its contempt powers and the legislature with its privileges stand on different footing. In this case the editor and the associate Editor of the Tamil Magazine "Nakkheeran" published from Madras moved the Hon'ble Supreme Court and asked for a writ restraining government officials from interfering with their right to publish the autobiography of Auto Shanker who had been convicted for several murders and awarded capital punishment. Auto Shanker had written his autobiography in jail which depicted close relationship between the prisoner and several IAS, IPS and other officials, some of whom were partners in several crimes. The announcement by the Magazine that very soon a sensational life history of Auto Shanker would be published created panic among several police officials that they might be exposed. They forced him by applying third degree method to write letter addressed to the Inspector General of Prisons that he had not written any such book and it should not be published. The I.G. wrote the publisher that it was false and should not be published.

It is to be noted that the petitioners did not show that they were authorized to publish the book the question for consideration was whether a citizen could prevent another for writing his autobiography. *Secondly,* does an authorized piece of writing infringe the citizen's right to privacy. Does the press have the right to publish an unauthorized account of a citizen's life. *Thirdly,* whether the Government could maintain an action for defamation or put restraint on press not to publish such materials against their officials or whether the officials themselves had the right to do so.

The Court held that the State or its officials have no authority in law to impose prior restraint on publication of defamatory matter. The public officials can take action only after the publication if it is found to be false.

In **State of Maharashtra v. Madhulkar Narain**,[47] it has been held that the *'right to privacy'* is available even to a woman of easy virtue and no one can invade her privacy. A police Inspector visited the house of one Banubai in uniform and demanded to have sexual intercourse with her. On refusing he tried to have her by force. She raised a hue and cry. When he was prosecuted he told the court that she was a lady of easy virtue and therefore her evidence was not to be relied. The Court rejected the argument of the applicant and held him liable for violating her right to privacy under Article 21 of the Constitution.

---

[47]   AIR 1991 SC 207

In a **landmark judgment**,[48] a two Judge Bench of the Madras High Court held that a minor girl had the right to bear a Child. In this case a 16 year old minor girl, Sashikala became pregnant and wanted to have the child against the opposition from her father. The father had filed a case in the Court seeking permission to have the pregnancy medically terminated on the ground that she was legally and otherwise also too young to take the decision to bear the child. It was argued that this would be detriment to the health of the minor mother and the child born of minor mother and also have wider social consequences. On the other hand, the public prosecutor, defending the case of the girl had argued that she had the right to bear the child under the broader "right to privacy". Even a minor had a right to privacy under Art.21 of the Constitution. He argued that the Indian Constitution does make any distinction between "minor" and "major" in so far as fundamental rights were concerned. He argued that Sashikala was a mature minor who is fully conscious of the consequences of bearing and delivering the Child. The Court accepted that Shashikala was Minor but did not agree with the petitioner's father, that the delivery in the case of minors was fraught with dangerous medical consequences. "The younger the mother; the better the birth" the Judges said. On the other hand, termination of the first pregnancy could lead to sterility. Quoting extensively from English and American Law and an American decision the bench held that in the case of a mature and understanding minor the opinion of the parent or guardian was not relevant. The Judges also quoted chapter

---

48   The Hindustan Times. 3-12-1993

and verse from Christian, Islamic and Hindu texts to show that destruction of human life even in the mother's womb had no moral sanction.

In **All India Imam Organization v. Union of India,**[49] the Hon'ble Supreme Court has held Imams who are in-charge of religious activities of Mosque are entitled to emoluments even in absence of statutory provisions in the wakfActj, 1954 in a number of cases it has been held that right to if enshrined in Article 21 means right to live with human dignity. The court did not accept the contention of the wakf Board that since Imams perform religious duties they are not entitled to any emoluments. Whatever may have the ancient concept but it has undergone a change and even Muslim countries Mosques are subsidized and the Imams are paid their remuneration. Therefore the submission that in our set up or in absence of any statutory provision in the wakf Act they are not entitled to any remuneration cannot be accepted. Financial difficulties of the institution cannot be above fundamental right of a citizen. If the Boards have been vested with responsibility of supervising and administering the wakf then it is their duty to arrange resources to pay Wakf Board to prepare a scheme for determining the remuneration of Imams of various categories of Mosques and finding out sources of income necessary for the purpose. This should be completed within six months.

---

[49]   AIR 1993 SC 2086

In **Mr. 'X' v. Hospital 'Z'**[50], the Hon'ble Supreme Court has held that although the "right to privacy" is a fundamental right under Art. 21 of the Constitution but it is not an absolute right and restrictions can be imposed on it for the prevention of crime, disorder or protection of health or morals or protection of rights and freedom of others. In this case the appellant after obtaining the degree of MBBS in 1987 joined the Nagaland State Medical and Health Service as Assistant Surgeon Grade I. A government servant was suffering from some disease. He was advised to go to the 'Z' hospital at Madras. The appellant was directed by the government of Nagaland to accompany the said patient to Madras for treatment. For the treatment of the disease the patient needed blood. The appellant was asked by the doctors to donate blood for the patient. When his blood samples were taken the doctors found that the appellant's blood group was (HIV) (Aids). In the meantime the appellant settled his marriage with one Miss 'Y' which was to be held on Dec. 12, 1995. But the marriage was called off on the ground that the blood test of the appellant conducted by the respondent's hospital was found to be HIV (+). As a result of this, he contended that his prestige among his family members was damaged. The appellant filed a writ petition in the High Court of Bombay for damages against the respondents on the ground that the information which was required to be secret under Medical Ethics was disclosed illegally and therefore the respondents were liable to pay damages. He contended that the respondents were under a duty to maintain confidentiality on account of Medical

---

[50]   AIR 1999 SC 495

Ethics formulated by the Indian medical Council. He contended that the appellant's "right to privacy" had been infringed by the respondents by disclosing that the appellant was HIV(+), and 'therefore' they are liable in damages.

A two judge division Bench of the Hon'ble Supreme Court comprising of Saghir Ahmad and Kripal, JJ., held that by disclosing that the appellant was suffering from AIDS the doctors had not violated the right of privacy of the appellant guaranteed by Art. 21. The Court held that although the right to privacy is a fundamental right under Art. 21, but it is not an absolute right and restrictions can be imposed on it. The right to marry is an essential element of right to privacy but is not absolute. Marriage is the sacred union, legally permissible, of two healthy bodies of opposite sexes. Every system of matrimonial law provides that if a person is suffering from venereal disease in a communicable form it will be open to the other partner in the marriage to seek divorce. If a person is suffering from that disease even prior to the marriage he has no right to marry so long as he is not fully unsecured of the decease. As such when the patient was found to be HIV(+), the disclosure by the Doctor was not violative of either the rule of confidentiality or the patient's right to privacy as the lady with whom the patient was likely to be married was saved by such disclosure of else she too would have been infected with the dreadful disease if marriage had taken place.

Miss Y was entitled to enjoy all human rights available to any other human being. This is apart from, and in addition to the fundamental right available to her under Art.21, which guarantees right to life to every citizen of the country. Right to life of the lady with whom the patient was to marry positively includes the right to be told that a person with whom she was proposed to be married was victim of a deadly disease which was sexually communicable. Right to life includes right to lead a healthy life so as to enjoy all faculties of the human body in their prime condition. Moreover, where there is a clash of two Fundamental Rights to life and his proposed wife's right to lead a healthy life which is her Fundamental Rights under Art. 21 the right which would advance the public morality or public interest would alone be enforced through the process of Court. The Court said that moral considerations cannot be kept at bay and the judges are not expected to sit as mute structures of clay in the hall, known as Court Room, but have to be sensitive, "*in the sense that they must keep their fingers firmly upon the pulse of the accepted morality of the day.*"

In **Ms X v. Mr. Z**[51], the wife filed a petition for dissolution of marriage on the ground of cruelty against husband under Section 10 of Divorce Act. The husband also asserted that his wife had adulterous affairs with one person which resulted in family way. The pregnancy of wife was terminated at All India Institute of Medical Science and records and slides of tabular gestation were preserved in hospital. The husband filed an application for seeking DNA test of the said slides with a view to ascertain if the husband is the father of the foetus. The Court held that the right to privacy, though a fundamental right forming part of right to life enshrined under Art. 21, is not an absolute right. When the right to privacy has become a part of a public document,

---

[51]   (1998) 8 SCC 296

in that case a person cannot insist that such DNA test would infringe his or her right to privacy. The foetus was no longer a part of body and when it has been preserved in AIMS the wife who has already discharged the same cannot claim that it affects her right of privacy. When adultery has been alleged to be one of the grounds of divorce in such circumstances the application of the husband seeking DNA test of the said slides can be allowed.

Supreme Court Advocates –on- record- association and ors. Vs Union of India 16.10.2015[52]

In the landmark judgement of the Supreme Court in laying down the NJAC as unconstitutional, the Supreme Court weighed the right to know against the right to information. During this discourse, the Supreme Court observed that the NJAC was in violation of the right to know as mere voluntarily supplication of information by the candidates, who are in the public sphere, does not waive their right to privacy. It was further opined that the balance between the two rights must be maintained adequately, and that the NJAC fails to achieve this balance.

The Bombay Mutton Dealer Association and Ors. Vs State of Maharashtra and Ors.[53]

Facts: The issue pertained to the ban of slaughtering and sale of meat on specified days of the jain festival Paryurshan.

---

[52]   2015 (11) SCALE1
[53]

Analysis: While discussing the various aspects of this case, The Supreme Court reaffirmed the *opinion juris* of *Hinsa Virodhak Sangh Vs Mirzapur Moti Kuresh Jamat*[54] and said that the personal eating habits of an individual is a part of his right to privacy which is included in Article 21 of the constitution.

K.S. Puttaswamy (Retd.) and Ors. Vs. Union of India and Ors.[55]

Facts: The case concerned the violation of the right to privacy by the Unique Identitfication Authority of India while collecting biometric data for issuance of the Aadhaar Card.

Issue: The collection of such biometric data was a violation of the right to privacy of citizens under Article 21 of the constitution. Held: While discussing the observations made in M.P. Sharma v. Satish Chandra and Kharak Singh v. State of U.P., the court said that there exists some uncertainty regarding the position of the right to privacy under the Indian Constitution and this must be clarified by either asserting the judgements in the aforementioned cases or be examined by a bigger bench of the court to be authoritatively decided once and for all.

---

54   [2008] INSC 467
55   (2015) 8 SCC 735

Anurima vs. Sunil Mehta[56] (MP HC)

Issue: Whether recorded private conversation of wife violated her right to privacy and was admissible as evidence

Facts: The husband filed for restitution of conjugal rights and submitted in evidence the conversation of the wife and one other person.

Held: The court while holding the evidence as inadmissible observed that the recording of private conversations of a wife were tantamount to an infringement of her right to privacy and placed reliance on PUCL vs Union of India[57] to observe that the right to privacy is a part of the right to life. It was further observed that the right to privacy would also encompass telephonic conversations in the privacy of home or office.

Union of India vs D.S. Meena[58]

Issue: Whether confidential reports regarding public servants could be divulged for the RTI? How to balance the public interest *vis a vis* right to privacy?

Facts: The respondent had filed an RTI for the Annual Confidential Reports of the third party which was granted by the CIC. The UOI appealed against this order of the CIC.

---

[56]   MANU/MP/0620/2015
[57]   AIR 1997 SC 568
[58]   2015 (150) DRJ97

Held : The court delved into the question of right to privacy of a person holding public office and reaffirmed the decision in *Kameshwar Prasad v. State of Bihar*[59] to state that the right to privacy of persons is not subsumed by them merely holding a public office. It was further observed that though the right to privacy of persons holding public office can be infringed in the furtherance of larger public interest, this public interest must be clear and evident from the request in order for the court to be inclined to infringe the right to privacy.

Ram Jethmalani and Ors. Vs. Union of India and Ors.[60]

Facts: The petition was regarding unaccounted monies allegedly lying in swiss bank accounts. The petitioner was seeking access to the information regarding individuals whose names were there in the CBI SIT report.

Issue: Whether the UOI could refuse to divulge such information on the ground of Right to Privacy.

Held: The court upheld that the general diaspora has a right to know and largely compelled the state to disclose the information to the petitioners. They observed that the right to privacy is a fundamental part of the right to life, and that it is imperative that persons are allowed pockets of freedom which are free from the scrutiny of the public unless the individuals act in an unlawful manner. The court, going

---

[59]   AIR 1962 SC 1166

[60]   (2011) 8 SCC 1

on to protect the right to privacy of individuals with bank accounts in swiss banks held that the government cannot reveal bank accounts without *prima facie* establishing wrong doing on the parts of such individuals.

Right to Privacy Studied in the Light of Various Other Rights

VIRGINITY TEST VIOLATES RIGHT TO PRIVACY UNDER ARTICLE 21

In **Surjit Singh Thind v. Kanwaljit Kaur**[61], the Punjab and Haryana High Court has held that allowing medical examination of a woman for her virginity amounts to violation of her right to privacy and personal liberty enshrined under Article 21 of the Constitution. In this case the wife has filed a petition for a decree of nullity of marriage on the ground that the marriage has never been consummated because the husband was impotent. The husband had taken the defense that the marriage was consummated and he was not impotent. In order to prove that the wife was not virgin the husband filed an application for her medical examination. The Court held that allowing the medical examination of a woman's virginity violates her right to privacy under Article 21 of the Constitution. Such an order would amount to roving enquiry against al female who is vulnerable even otherwise. The virginity test cannot constitute the sole basis, to prove the consummation of marriage.

---

[61] AIR 2003 P H 353

In **Malak Singh v. State of Punjab,**[62] the question was whether a person whose name was included in the surveillance register had right of opportunity to be heard before such inclusion. While the Court held that the rule of natural justice was not attracted but it made the law on the subject clear and laid down the guidelines regarding the mode of surveillance by the police. It held the under Section 23 of the Punjab Police Act it was the duty of the police officers to keep surveillance over bad characters, and habitual offenders for the purpose of preventing crimes. So long as surveillance is for the purposes of prevention of crimes and confined to the limits prescribed by Rule 23 (7) of the Punjab Police Rule, a person cannot complain against the inclusion of his name in the surveillance register. But if it is excessive and goes beyond the limits prescribed by Rule, i.e., surveillance of a person who does not belong to above categories, its validity may be challenged as infringing the right of privacy of a citizen as his fundamental right to personal liberty under Article 21 and freedom of movement in Article 19(1)(d). In the instant case, on the basis of the relevant records the Court was satisfied that there was sufficient ground for the inclusion of the relevant records the Court was satisfied that there was sufficient ground for the inclusion of the petitioner's name in the surveillance register.

A detenu can be subjected only to such restrictions on his personal liberty as authorized by or under the law of preventing detention and imposition of any unauthorized restriction, therefore, will violate Article 21. For example,

---

[62]   AIR 1981 SC 760

in **State of Maharashtra v. Prabhakar Pandurang**,[63] the petitioner was detained in jail under the Preventive Detention Act. He wrote a scientific book in prison and sought permission from the Government to send it to his wife for publication. The Government refused permission to him. The Court held that this was an infringement of his personal liberty as the restriction was not authorized by the preventive Detention Act.

RIGHT TO PRIVACY SEARCH AND SEIZURES:

M.P. Sharma v. Statish Chandra,[64]was the first case before the Hon'ble Supreme Court wherein the court had the opportunity of considering the constitutional status of right to privacy in the context of state power of search and seizure. The point for consideration was whether the state power of search and seizure under Section 96 Criminal Procedure Code, 1898 (Application to High Court to set aside declaration of forfeiture) violated individual rights to privacy which may be read in Articles 19(1)(b)(To assemble peaceably and without arms) and 20(3) (No person accused of any offence shall be compelled to be a witness against himself) of the Constitution. Eight judges of the Hon'ble Supreme Court unanimously held that search by itself was not a restriction on the right to hold and enjoy property. The Court speaking through Jagannadhadas, J. held that when the Constitution makers thought fit not to subject such regulation toconstitutional limitations by recognizing

---

63   AIR 1986 SC 424
64   AIR 1954 SC 300

of a fundamental right to privacy, analogousto the American Fourth Amendment which secures to the people the right to secure in their persons, houses, papers and effects against unreasonable search and seizures, we have no jurisdiction to import into a totally different fundamental right by some process of strained construction. In this manner the court missed a great opportunity of importing the right to privacy into the public law.

RIGHT TO PRIVACY AND SURVEILLANCE:

The question whether the right to privacy is included within the expressionof personal liberty was directly raised before the Hon'ble Supreme Court in **Kharak Singh v. State of U. P.**[65] The sole question for determination was whether 'surveillance' under Chapter XX of the U. P. Police Regulations constituted an infringement of any of citizen's fundamental rights guaranteed by Part III of the Constitution. In his case the petitioner was a person accused of the offence of dacoity. After his release he was put under police surveillance. This power of police surveillance was challenged by the petitioner on the ground that the U. P. Police Regulation 236 authorizing such surveillance is violative of Article 19(1) (d) (To move freely throughout the territory of India) and Article 21 of the Constitution. The government justified the exercise of the power on the ground that it is exercised only against those who are suspected to be of proved anti-social habits and tendencies in the interest of the protection of the society from these elements. The issue

---

[65]   AIR 1963 SC 1295

whether right to privacy is included in Article 21 was also directly raised. N. RajagopalaAyyangar, J. speaking for the majority of the court held that the right to privacy is not a guaranteed right under the Constitution and therefore, the attempt to restrain the movements of an individual which is merely a mariner in which privacy is invaded is not an infringement of any fundamental right guaranteed by Part IN of the Constitution. No matter the court showed an awareness to the right to privacy when Ayanger, J. highlighted the lack of provision in the Constitution of India like those of Fourth Amendment of the American Constitution. The court conceded that the common law maxim *'et domussuachiqueesttussimumrefugiurn'* (every man's house is his castle) lays down the right valued most by civilized men. But at that time the court was not prepared to give wide meaning to the expression 'personal liberty' in Article 21 as to include within it the right to privacy.

This residual and halting approach of the apex court is not giving a constitutional status to the right to privacy provoked SubhaRao, J. to write a forceful dissent. The learned judge though conceded that the Constitution of India does not expressly declare a right to privacy as fundamental right, but observed that the said right is an essential ingredient of personal liberty. SubhaRao, J., supporting his views by citing Frankfurter, J. in **Wolf v. Colorado,**[66] further observed that every democratic society sanctifies domestic life; it is expected to give him rest, physical happiness, peace of mind and security. In the last resort a person's house, where he lives with his family is his

---

[66] (1948) 338 US 25

'castle', it is rampart against encroachment of his personal liberty. He further observed that the right to personal liberty guaranteed by the Constitution of India encompasses not only the right to move about the county, but also to be free from encroachments on personal liberty and accordingly held that surveillance was unconstitutional.

A decade later, the above consideration was judicially recognised in **Gobind v. State of M.P.**[67] The three Judges Bench of the Hon'ble Supreme Court unanimously speaking through Mathew, J. revitalized and extended the minority opinion of SubhaRao, J. in Kharak Singh's case asserting the right of privacy of individual citizens. In this case the facts were similar to that of Kharak Sigh's case. The police had put the petitioner under surveillance and were making domiciliary visit both by day and night at frequent intervals and secretly picketing his house and watching his movements. The M. P. Police Regulations 855 and *856* authorizing such a surveillance was challenged before the Hon'ble Supreme Court as violating his right to privacy forming a part of freedom of movement guaranteed under Article 19(1)(d) (To move freely throughout the territory of India) and personal liberty under Article 21 of the Constitution. Mathew, J. cited authority from learned writings" and judicial opinion[40] from U.S.A in order to establish a separate zone of right to privacy under our Constitution and observed:

"There can be no doubt that the maker of our Constitution wanted to ensure conditions favorable to the pursuit of happiness. They certainly realized as Brandeis, J said in his

---

[67]   AIR 1975 SC 1378

dissent in Olmstead v. United States[68], the significance of man's spiritual nature, of his feelings and of his intellect and that only a part of the pain, pleasure, satisfaction of life can be found in material things and therefore, they must be deemed to have conferred upon the individual as against the government a sphere where he should be left alone."

Hence, the Hon'ble Supreme Court for the first time in India located a separate zone of right to privacy in the Constitution of India emanating from the freedom of speech and expression, Article 19(I) (a); freedom of movement, Article 19(1)(d) and right to personal liberty, Article 21. After firmly bestowing a constitutional status on right to privacy, the learned Judge was quick to and that like any other fundamental right, this right is also not absolute, and could be subjected to reasonable restrictions on the basis of compelling state interest. The court allowed domiciliary surveillance of suspected criminals but gave note of caution that such provision can be held valid only when it is supported by material fact that the suspects are addicted to, such crimes as to "involve public peace and security and they are dangerous to security risks."

Govind's case is certainly a pace-setter value judgment because it shows an awareness to the sacred privacy-dignity claims of the people of India by protecting individual autonomy which is the central concern of any system of limited government by plugging all subtle and far-reaching means of invading privacy which makes it possible to be heard in the street what is whispered in the closet.

---

[68]   277 U.S. 438 (1928)

RIGHT TO PRIVACY – SEXUAL AUTONOMY OF WOMEN

In Re- Ratanmala, the right to privacy even of a prostitute was recognized as an important right. The behaviour of a police officer who, while raiding a brothel, proceeded to the bed room of a girl, and pushed open the door even without the civility of a knock to prepare her for the intrusion, was accordingly held legally inexcusable. Similarly, in **State of Maharashtra v. Madhulkar Narain,**[69] it has been held that the 'right to privacy' is available to a woman of easy virtue and no one can invade her privacy. In the present case, a Police Inspector visited the house of one Banubai in uniform and demanded to have sexual intercourse with her. On refusing he tried to have her by force. She raised a hue and cry. When he was prosecuted he told the court that she was a lady of easy virtue and therefore, her evidence was not to be relied. The court rejected the argument of the applicant and held him liable for violating her right to privacy under Article 21 of the Constitution. Further the Hon'ble Supreme Court in **State of Punjab v. Gurmit Singh**[70]**,"** held that a woman of easy virtue also could not be raped by a person for that reason. The Hon'ble Supreme Court observed that "Even if the prosecutrix has been promiscuous in her sexual behavior earlier, she has right to refuse to submit herself to sexual intercourse to anyone and everyone because she is not a vulnerable object or prey for being sexually assaulted by anyone and everyone.".

---

[69]   Supra 64
[70]   AIR 1996 SC 1393

RIGHT TO PRIVACY BASED ON NATURAL MODESTY AND MORALITY

In **Neera Mathur v. Life Insurance Corporation of India**[71], the Hon'ble Supreme Court held that a declaration from requiring details of personal problems from lady applicant was indeed embarrassing, if not humiliating. Modesty and self respect may perhaps preclude disclosure of such personal problems like whether her menstrual period is regular or painless, the number of conception taken place, how many have gone full terms etc. The respondent was directed to delete such columns and the practice of including such questions in declaration forms was deprecated. In **Nihal Chand v. Bhagwan Dei**[72], the Allahabad High Court while emphasizing the importance of right to privacy, observed that the right to privacy is based on natural modesty and human morality. It is not confined to any class, creed, colour and is very sacred.

TELEPHONE TAPPING AND RIGHT TO PRIVACY

Individuals, politicians, professionals, officials and others talk a lot in private over telephone. It is gross invasion of everything that is talked on telephone by them is tapped and published in public forums. Except for the reasons of public safety or security of the nation or for the detection and prevention of serious crimes, a State cannot have

---

[71] (1992) 1 SCC 286
[72] AIR 1935 All 1002

any lawful excuse to invade human privacy. Without any reasonable cause or justification neither the state nor any private individual can legally claim to have any right to intercept telephonic communication of any person. In a democratic country, telephone-tapping without any lawful excuse at the behest of the government, Central or State, is far more deplorable than telephonic-tapping by a private individual. A man feels loss of his privacy i.e. loss of his personal liberty when he comes to know that his telephonic talk is being tapped by somebody. Every individual should have a free private zone. His ideas, thoughts, beliefs, views, etc. should be inviolable. There are certain provisions in different legislations which permits interception of any communication sent by telegraph or any postal article on the occurrence of any public emergency or in the interest of the public safety or tranquility." The Law Commission has observed in its Forty-Second Report, 1971, "As the law on the subject is still rudimentary even in advanced countries, we would not advice comprehensive legislation to deal with all aspects of invasion of privacy. It is better to make a beginning with those invasions which may amount to what is known as eavesdropping and unauthorized publication of photographs and' leave the rest to be considered later on in the light of the experience gained and legislation introduced."[73]

Telephone-tapping is a serious invasion of the right to privacy. One can tap the telephone lines and listen to others talking. Some persons may use it for their personal pleasure,

---

[73] Prof. M.P. Jain, "Constitutional Law of India", Wadhwa and Company Nagpur, (2007), p.1134

some for commercial gains and we find the Government using it on the pretext of surveillance. In all these instances, right to privacy was the victim. There is however, no express guarantee against the telephone-tapping under the Constitution of India. The challenge to telephone-tapping under Article 21 was first considered in **R. M. Malkani v. State of Maharashtra**[74]. In this case, the telephonic conversation between two parties was tape-recorded by the police with the consent of one of the parties. The Hon'ble Supreme Court observed that the conversation could be used in evidence as it was voluntary and there was no duress or compulsion to extract the same. The fact that the tape-recording instrument was attached without appellant's knowledge does not make the conversation inadmissible against him. The Hon'ble Supreme Court further observed that it would not tolerate safeguards for the protection of citizen to be imperiled by permitting the police to proceed by unlawful or irregular methods. At the same time the court held that even stolen evidence was admissible if it was not tainted by an inadmissible confess of guilt.

In **Peoples Union for Civil Liberties v. Union of India**[75]**,**" the Hon'ble Supreme Court examined in detail the challenge to the right to privacy by way of telephone tapping. The court looked into the constitutional validity of Section 5(2) of the Indian Telegraph Act, 1885, by virtue of which the government has tapped some telephonic conversations. After holding that privacy is an essential ingredient of personal liberty, Kuldeep Singh, J. came to

---

[74]   AIR 1973 SC 157

[75]   1995 SCALE (2) 542

the conclusion that telephone tapping is a serious invasion of the individual's privacy. He observed that with the growth of highly sophisticated communication technology, the right to hold telephone conversation in the privacy of one's home or office without interference is increasingly susceptible to abuse. It has held that telephone tapping, a form of 'technological eavesdropping' infringed the right to privacy. Finding that the government had failed to lay down the proper procedure under Section 7(2) (b) of the Act to ensure procedural safeguards against the misuse of the power under Section 5(2), the court prescribed stringent measure to protect the individual's privacy to the extent possible.

TELEPHONE-TAPPING: AN INVASION ON RIGHT TO PRIVACY.

In a historic judgment in **People's Union for Civil Liberties v. Union of India**,[76] popularly known as *'Phone Tapping case'.* The Hon'ble Supreme Court has held that telephone tapping is a serious invasion of an individual's right to privacy which is part of the right to "life and personal liberty" enshrined under Art. 21 of the Constitution, and it should not be resorted to by the State unless there is public emergency or interest of public safety squires. The petition was filed by way of public interest litigation under Art.32 of the Constitution by the People's Union of Civil Liberties – a voluntary organization – highlighting the incidents of telephone tapping in the recent years. The petitioners has

---

[76] Supra 4

challenged the constitutional validity of Section 5 of the Indian Telegraph Act, 1885 which authorizes the Central or State Government to resort to phone tapping in the circumstances mentioned therein. The writ petition was filed in the wake of the report on "Tapping of Politicians Phones" by the Central Bureau of Investigation (CBI).

The Court laid down exhaustive guidelines to regulate the discretion vested in the State under Section 5 of the Indian Telegraph Act for the purposes of telephone tapping and interception of other messages so as to safeguard public interest against arbitrary and unlawful exercise of power by the Government. The Court has expressed displeasure that the State has so far not framed rules to prevent misuse of the poser. In the absence of just and fair procedure for regulating the exercise of power under Section 5(2) of the Indian Telegraph Act, it is not possible to safeguard the rights of citizens guaranteed under Arts. 9(1)(a) and 21 of the Constitution. The CBI investigations have revealed several lapses in the execution of the orders passed by the State while exercising power under the Act. Section 5(2) of the Act permits the interception of messages in accordance with the provisions of the Act. "Occurrence of any public emergency" or in the interest of public safety" are the *sine qua non* "for the application of the provisions under Section 5(2) of the Act unless a public emergency has occurred or the interest of public safety demands, the authorities have no jurisdiction to exercise the powers under the said legislation. The Court said public emergency would mean the prevailing of sudden condition or state-of-affairs affecting the people at large calling for immediate action. The expression 'public safety' means the state or condition of grave danger or risk for the people at large. When either these two conditions are not in existence the Court said. The Central Government or the State Government or the authorized officers cannot resort to telephone tapping even though there is satisfaction that it is necessary or expedient so to do in the interest of sovereignty and integrity of the country. In other orders, even if the Central Government is satisfied that it is necessary or expedient so to do in the interest of the sovereignty or integrity of the country or the security of the State or friendly relations with foreign States or public order of for preventing for incitements to the commission of an offence it cannot intercept the massage or resort to telephone tapping *unless a public emergency* has occurred or the interest of public safety or the existence of the interest of public safety requires.

The Court has laid down the following procedural safeguards for the exercise of power under Section 5(2) of the Indian Telegraph Act –

(1) An order for telephone tapping can be issued only by the Home Secretary of the Central Government or the State Governments. In an urgent case, the power may be delegated to an officer of the Home Department of the Central and State Governments not below the rank of Joint Secretary.

(2) The copy of the order shall be sent to the Review Committee within one week of the passing of order.

(3) The order shall, unless renewed, cease to have effect at the end of two months from the date of issue. The authority making the order may review before that

period if it considered that it is necessary to continue the order in terms of Section 5(2) of the Act.

(4) The authority issuing the order shall maintain the records of intercepted communications, the extent the material to be disclosed number of persons, their identity to whom the material is disclosed.

(5) The use of the intercepted material shall be limited to the minimum that is necessary in terms of Section 5(2) the Act.

(6) The Review Committee shall on its own, within two months, investigate whether there is or has been a relevant order under Section 5(2) of the Act.

(7) If on investigation the Review Committee concludes that there has been a contravention of the provisions of Section 5(2) of the Act, shall set aside the order. It can also direct the destruction the copies of the intercepted material.

(8) If on investigation the Review Committee comes the conclusion that there has been no contravention of the relevant provision of the Act, it shall record the finding to that effect.

The judgment of the Hon'ble Supreme Court delivered by a Division Bench comprising Mr. Justice Kuldeep Singh and Mr. Justice S. Sagir Ahmad will go a long way in protecting the right of privacy of Indian citizens and others enshrined under Art. 21 of the Constitution. The Court noted that with the growth of highly sophisticated communication technology the right to hold telephone conversation in the privacy of one's home or office without interference is increasingly susceptible to abuse.

In **LIC of India v. Consumer Education & Research Centre**,[77] it has been held that the "right to life and livelihood" as interpreted in **Olga Tellis v. Bombay Municipal Corporation**[78]and several other cases by this Court includes the 'right to life insurance policies of LIC of India' and it must be within the paying capacity and means of the insured. The Preamble chapter on Fundamental Rights and directive principles accord right to livelihood as a meaningful life, social security and disablement benefits are integral scheme of socio-economic justice to the people, in particular to the middle class and lower middle class and all affordable people. Life insurance coverage is against disablement or in the event of death of the insured, economic support for the dependants, social security to livelihood of the insured or the dependants. The appropriate life insurance policy within the paying capacity and means of the insured to pay pariah is one of the social security measures envisaged under the Constitution to make right of life meaningful, worth living and right to livelihood a means for substance. In that case the conditions imposed and denial to accept policies under Table 58 was challenged by the respondent as violative of right to life in Art. 21 of the Constitution. The Hon'ble Supreme Court held that the terms and conditions imposed by the LIC for accepting policy must be just, fair and reasonable. The policy cannot be restricted only to salaried class in Government service or quasi Government

---

[77] (1995) 5 SCC 482

[78] Supra 5

bodies or reputed commercial firms. The Court held that such a condition is unconstitutional. However, since Table 58 is severable from rest of the condition the Court held that whole of Table 58 need not be declared unconstitutional.

In **Pragati Varghese v. Cyril George Varghese**[79] Mumbai High Court has struck down Section 10 the Indian Divorce Act, 1869 under which a Christian wife had to prove adultery along with cruelty or desertion while seeking a divorce on the ground that it violates the fundamental right of Christian women guaranteed under Articles 21, 15 and 14 of the Constitution. The Court also struck down Sections 17 and 20 of the Act which stipulated that an annulment or divorce passed by a district Court needed to be confirmed by a 3 Judges Bench of the High Court. The Court held Section 10 compels the wife, who has been deserted or treated with cruelty, to continue her life with a man she hates... Such a life is sub-human. There is denial to dissolve the marriage when the marriage has broken down irretrievably.

PRIVACY AND RESTITUTION OF CONJUGAL RIGHTS:

Fundamental Rights jurisprudence witnessed another development in the first half of 1980's wherein constitutionality of Section 9 of Hindu Marriage Act, 1955 providing for restitution of conjugal rights was challenged on the ground of violation of Article 21 in **T. Sareetha v. T.**

---

[79]   AIR 1997 Bom. 349

VenkataSubbaih[80]. The court declared Section 9 as *ultra vires* and violative of Articles 14 and 21 of the Constitution. **Chaudhary, J.** While examining restitution of conjugal rights in relation to right to personal liberty opined:

A decree of restitution of conjugal rights constitutes the grossest form of violation of an individual's right to privacy. It denies women her choice whether, when and how, her body is to become the vehicle for the procreation of another human being. Justice Chaudhary has no hesitation in characterizing the remedy of restitution of conjugal rights as a savage and barbarous remedy, violating the right to privacy and human dignity guaranteed by Article 21 of our Constitution.

The issue again cropped up in **Harvinder Kaur v. Harminder Singh**[81] Justice Avadh Bihari Rohtagi of Delhi High Court has expressed a contrary view and upheld the validity of Section 9 of the Hindu Marriage Act. The court opined that though sex constitutes an important element in marriage but it does not constitute the sole object. Court opposed the introduction of constitutional principles in the privacy of a home. The court observed that in the privacy of a home Articles 21 and 14 have no place whatsoever, matrimonial relations are rather based on love, affection, care and the like considerations.

The Hon'ble Supreme Court finally set the controversy at rest in **Saroj Rani v. Sudarshan Kumar**[82] by approving

---

[80]   AIR 1983 AP 356
[81]   AIR 1984 Del 66
[82]   AIR 1984 SC 1562

the judgment of Delhi High Court in **Harvinder Kaur's case**[83]. The Hon'ble Supreme Court ruled that Section 9 serves social purpose as an aid to the preservation of marriage and therefore satisfies Articles 14 and 21. However, unfortunately the Hon'ble Supreme Court did not consider the question of wife's right to privacy. The court was influenced by the method of execution of the decree of restitution of conjugal rights.

RIGHT TO PRIVACY OF HIV INFECTED PEOPLE:

Another dimension of right to privacy i.e. right to privacy of AIDS infected people has received judicial attention during the recent times. The question here arises is whether AIDS infected people have a right to privacy i.e. whether they have right that their HIV should be kept secret. The question has acquired immense importance in the present time. It will not be an exaggeration to say that the wholecommunity is sitting on AIDS bomb ready to explode anytime. In view of this, it is pertinent to examine the right to privacy in AIDS infected people.

In Mr.'**X**' v. Hospital '**Z**'[84], the Hon'ble Supreme Court was seized on an issue concerning an AIDS patient and his right to privacy and confidentiality regarding his medical condition, and the right of the lady to whom he was engaged to lead a healthy life. The Hon'ble Supreme Court was of

---

[83]   Supra 90
[84]   Supra 67

the opinion that the life of the fiancée would be endangered by her marriage and consequent conjugal relations with the AIDS victim, and consequently she was entitled to information regarding the medical condition of the man she was to marry.

In a recent case of **Sharda v. Dharampal**[85], the Hon'ble Supreme Court was confronted with the issue whether subjecting a person to a medical test be in violation of Article 21 of the Constitution. The court outlined the concept of the law of privacy in India and was of the opinion that the right to privacy in terms of Article 21 of the Constitution is not an absolute right.

---

[85]   AIR 2003 SC 3450

STATUTORY PROVISIONS FOR SAFEGUARD OF PRIVACY

India does not currently have a sui-generis statute that safeguards privacy horizontally across different contexts. However various statutes dealing with issues as diverse as banking and finance, professional ethics of lawyers, doctors and chartered accountants, information technology and telephony etc contain provisions which either explicitly or impliedly protect privacy or offer victims remedies for their breach.

It is interesting to note that legal developments in the field of privacy have been unable to keep a score with the advancement in the technology. No country, till date, specifically lists out the right to privacy as a specific and absolute constitutional right. The evolution of Privacy law is attributable to judicial pronouncements made by various courts. Despite the lack of specific constitutional recognition, the right to privacy has long held a place in international documents on human rights such as Article 12 of the Universal Declaration of Human Rights, 1948. Article 17 of the International Covenant on Civil and Political Rights, 1966 to which India is a signatory, reads as follows:

i. No one shall be subject to arbitrary or unlawful interference with his privacy, family, home or correspondence, nor to lawful attacks on his honour and reputation.

ii. Everyone has the right to the protection of the law against such interference or attacks.

Article 8 of the European Convention on Human Rights reads as follows:

i. Everyone has the right to respect for his private and family life, his home and his correspondence.

ii. There shall be no interference by a public authority with the exercise of this right, except such as is in accordance with law and is necessary in a democratic society in the interests of national security, public safety, for the prevention of disorder and crime or for the protection of health or morals.

The Information Technology Act 2000 contains a number of provisions which can be used to safeguard against online/computer related privacy. The Act provides for civil and criminal liability with respect to hacking (Sec. 43 & 66) and imprisonment of up to three years with fine for electronic voyeurism (Sec. 66E), Phishing and identity theft (Sec. 66C/66D), Offensive email (Sec. 66A). Disclosure by the government of information obtained in the course of exercising its interception powers under the IT Act is punishable with imprisonment of up to two years and fine (Sec. 72)[86] Section 72A of the IT Act penalizes the unauthorized disclosure of "personal information" by any person who has obtained such information while providing services under a lawful contract. Such disclosure must be made with the intent of causing wrongful loss or obtaining a wrongful gain and is punishable with imprisonment which may extend to 3 years or a fine of Rs. 500,000 or both.

In addition to these sections, the Act also contains provisions with respect to Data Protection which are described below.

Data Protection Liability for 'body-corporates' under Section 43A of the Information Technology Act and the Reasonable Security Practices Rules 2011

Section 43A of the IT Act, newly introduced in 2008, makes a start at introducing a mandatory data protection regime in Indian law. The section obliges corporate bodies who 'possess, deal or handle' any 'sensitive personal data' to implement and maintain 'reasonable security practices', failing which, they would be liable to compensate those affected by any negligence attributable to this failure. Highlights of these provisions are:

---

[86]   For a more elaborate treatment of the IT Act's protections of privacy, and the manner in which they have been used, See Prashant Iyengar, *Privacy and the Information Technology Act in India*, SSRN ELIBRARY (2011), http://papers.ssrn.com/sol3/papers.cfm?abstract_id=1807575 (last visited Nov. 22, 2012)

- It is only the narrowly-defined 'body corporate'[87] engaged in 'commercial or professional activities' that are the targets of this section. Thus government agencies and non-profit organizations are entirely excluded from the ambit of this section.

- "Sensitive personal data or information" is any information that the Central Government may designate as such, when it sees fit to.

- The "reasonable security practices" which the section obliges body corporate to observe are restricted to such measures as may be specified either "in an agreement between the parties" or in any law in force or as prescribed by the Central Government.

In April 2011, the Ministry of Information and Technology, notified rules[88] under Section 43A in order to define "sensitive personal information" and to prescribe "reasonable security practices" that body corporate must observe in relation to the information they hold. By defining both phrases in terms that require executive elaboration, the section and the rules in effect pre-empt the courts from evolving an iterative, contextual definition of what would count as a reasonable security practice in relation to data.

---

[87] Section 43A defines "'body corporate" as any company and includes a firm, sole proprietorship or other association of individuals engaged in commercial or professional activities;

[88] The Information Technology (Reasonable security practices and procedures and sensitive personal information) Rules, 2011. Available at http://www.mit.gov.in/sites/upload_files/dit/files/GSR3_10511%281%29.pdf (last accessed November 15th, 2011

Sensitive Personal Information

Rule 3 of these Rules designates the following types of information as 'sensitive personal information':

i.   password;

2.   financial information such as Bank account or credit card or debit card or other payment instrument details;

iii. physical, physiological and mental health condition;

iv.   sexual orientation;

v.   medical records and history;

vi.   Biometric information;

vii. Any detail relating to the above clauses as provided to body corporate for providing service; and,

viii. any of the information received under above clauses by body corporate for processing, stored or processed under lawful contract or otherwise.

Prior Consent and Use Limitation during Data Collection

Body Corporate is forbidden by the rules from collecting sensitive personal information unless:

(a)   the information is collected for a lawful purpose connected with a function or activity of the agency;

(b) The collection of the information is necessary for that purpose.[89]

They and "any person" holding sensitive personal information are forbidden from "keeping that information for longer than is required for the purposes for which the information may lawfully be used", this however does not apply to "any information that is freely available or accessible in public domain or accessible under the Right to Information Act, 2005 or any other law for the time being in force.

Many other rules have similar provisions which the body corporate needs to follow. Moreover, non-compliance with such rules attracts civil liability.

Mascon Global Limited V. CCA, Google etc, disposed by the CAT on May 28, 2010, the appellant had sought details about an email account from Google which was purportedly being used to send defamatory emails. The CAT remanded the case to the Adjudicating Officer, which according to it was the appropriate forum to decide the case. 49 In another case, widely reported in the press, a man filed a complaint of hacking against his estranged wife alleging that she had, with the aid of her professional colleagues, hacked into his and his father's email account in order to obtain evidence in support of a dowry harassment case that she had filed against them.[90]

---

[89]   Rule 5 of the Rules

[90]   Mubarak Ansari, *Estranged wife hacks man's email*, SAKAL TIMES, August 25, 2011, http://www.sakaaltimes.com/

The Adjudicating Officer in the first instance had dismissed the complaint believing her assertion that the man and his father had themselves given her the password– a contention which was not denied by the complainant.

On appeal, however, the man contended that he had not, in fact, given his wife the password. The CAT ordered the case to be re-heard by the AO.[91] Although the complaint alleged 'hacking' by the woman, the case in fact refers to a privacy grievance of the complainant.

Criminal Complaints for privacy offences under the IT Act

No special procedure is prescribed for the trial of cyber offences and hence the general provisions of criminal procedure would apply with respect to investigation by the police, charge sheet, trial, decision, sentencing and appeal. Section 78 of the IT Act empowers police officers of the rank of Inspectors and above to investigate offences under the IT Act. Many States have set up dedicated Cyber Crime Police Stations to investigate offences under this Act. Thus, for example, the State of Karnataka has set up a special Cyber Crime police station that is responsible for investigating all

---

sakaaltimesbeta/20110825/4640115296625293785.htm (last visited Oct 3, 2011).

[91] Vinod Kaushik v. Madhvika Joshi, (2011), http://catindia.gov.in/pdfFiles/Appeal_No_2.pdf (last visited Nov 23, 2012).

offences under the IT Act with respect to the entire territory of Karnataka.[92]

Offences punishable with imprisonment up to 3 years are compoundable by a competent court.

However repeat offenders cannot have their subsequent offences compounded. Additionally, offences which "affect the socio-economic conditions of the country" or those committed against a child under 18 years of age or against women cannot be compounded.[93]

According to the latest (2009) statistics from the National Crime Records Bureau, there has been a steady rise in the number of complaints lodged and arrests made (both privacy and non-privacy related) with respect to offences under the IT Act.[94] In 2009, for instance, 420 complaints were registered, as against a figure of 288 for the previous year marking an increase of 41%. In the same period, the number of arrests made went up from 178 to 288 marking an increase of 41%.[95]

Of these, the NCBR categorizes 10 complaints in 2009 as pertaining to 'Breach of confidentiality/privacy' as against 9 complaints in the previous year, 5 arrests were made in

---

[92]   Home and Transport Secretariat, Notification no. HD 173 POP 99 Bangalore, Dated 13th September 2001
        Available at < http://cyberpolicebangalore.nic.in/pdf/notification_1.pdf>

[93]   Section 77A of the Information Technology Act.

[94]   CRIME IN INDIA - 2009, (2010), http://ncrb.nic.in/CII-2009-NEW/Compendium2009.pdf (last visited Nov. 23, 2012)

[95]   Supra.

2009 with respect to these offences. However this figure does not exhaust the number of privacy complaints in the country since, in many cases, violations of privacy may result from 'Hacking with a computer system' which, according to NCBR statistics, accounted for the largest number of complaints (233) and arrests (107) made under the IT Act in 2009.

Data Protection Act

In 1998, Britain enacted the Data Protection Act, which lays down the principles and establishes a hierarchy of officials. Data controllers are subject to the jurisdiction of the Information Commissioner. It says: "Data controllers must also abide by the data protection principles. They are, in brief, (a) the data must be processed fairly and lawfully and only for one of the prescribed purposes. For data concerning 'sensitive' matters, there is a narrower group of specified purposes; (b) it must be adequate, relevant and not excessive for the purpose; (c) it must be accurate, and where necessary, kept up to date; (d) it must not be kept for longer than is necessary; (e) it must be processed in accordance with the rights of data subjects; (f) appropriate technical and organizational measures must be taken against unauthorized or unlawful processing and against accidental loss or destruction of or damage to the data; (g) it must not be transferred out of the EEA [European Economic Area] unless the country to which it is taken or sent gives adequate protection for the rights of data subjects.

"The Commissioner can serve an enforcement notice if she is satisfied that a data controller has contravened any of these principles. An individual who suffers damage because a data controller has contravened any requirement of the Act is entitled to claim compensation. The special provisions for journalistic material gives exemption from: the data subjection principles (except those concerning security of data); data subject access rights; the rights of data subjects to prevent data processing; the rights of data subjects to correct inaccuracies; and rights concerning automated decision-making.[96]

Any law on data protection enacted by the Parliament of India will be tested on the anvil of Article 19. Section 32 of the British Data Protection Act provides "public interest" exemptions for "journalistic, literary or artistic material". The test in each case is public interest. Public interest is a concept entirely different from material in which the public would be interested.

In 2004, the Supreme Court of India decided a case in which the right to privacy was involved. It concerned Section 73 of the Indian Stamp Act, 1899, and its amendment by Andhra Pradesh in 1986. As amended in 1986, it read:

> "Every public officer or any person having in his custody any registers, books, records, papers, documents or proceedings, the inspection whereof may attend to secure any duty, or to prove or lead

---

[96] Media Law, by Geoffrey Robertson, QC and Andrew Nicol, QC, Penguin, 4th Edition, pg. 278-279.

to the discovery of any fraud or omission in relation to any duty, shall at all reasonable times permit any person authorized in writing by the Collector to enter upon any premises and to inspect for such purposes the registers, books, records, papers, documents and proceedings, and to take such notes and extracts as he may deem necessary, without fee or charge and if necessary to seize them and impound the same under proper acknowledgement.

"Provided that such seizure of any registers, books, records, papers, documents or other proceedings, in the custody of any bank be made only after a notice of 30 days to make good the deficit stamp duty is given."

The Supreme Court Bench, comprising R. Lahoti and A. Bhan, surveyed the case law in the U.S. and in India, but not in the U.K. It held:

"The impugned provision in Section 73 enabling the Collector to authorise 'any person' whatsoever in respect, to take notes or extracts from the papers in the public office suffers from the vice of excessive delegation as there are no guidelines in the Act and, more importantly, the Section allows the facts relating to the customer's privacy to reach non-governmental persons and would, on that basis, be an unreasonable encroachment into the customer's rights. This part of Section 73 permitting delegation to 'any person' suffers from the above serious defects and for that reason is, in our view, unenforceable.

> The state must clearly define the officers by designation or state that the power can be delegated to officers not below a particular rank in the official hierarchy, as may be designated by the state."

Besides, the AP amendment of 1986 permitted inspection being carried out by the Collector by having access to documents that were even in private custody; that is, custody other than that of a public officer. It empowered invasion of the home of the person in whose possession the documents "tending" to or leading to the various facts stated in Section 73 were in existence. Section 73 was devoid of any safeguards as to probable or reasonable cause or reasonable basis or materials. It, therefore, violated the right to privacy both of the house and of the person. The court referred to the R. Rajagopal case wherein the learned judges held that "the right to personal liberty also means life free from encroachments unsustainable in law", and such a right flowed from Article 21 of the Constitution.

Right to privacy was upheld again by the Supreme Court of India in another judgment most recently: Ram Jethmalani vs Union of India[97]. Delivered by Justices P. Sathasivam and H.L. Gokhale, it read:

> "Right to privacy is an integral part of right to life. This is a cherished constitutional value, and it is important that human beings be allowed domains of freedom that are free of public scrutiny unless they act in an unlawful manner.…. as constitutional

---

[97] No citation found. Excerpt taken from Internet

adjudicators we always have to be mindful of preserving the sanctity of constitutional values, and hasty steps that derogate from fundamental rights, whether urged by governments or private citizens, howsoever well meaning they may be, have to be necessarily very carefully scrutinized. The solution for the problem of abrogation of one zone of constitutional values cannot be the creation of another zone of abrogation of constitutional values.... An inquisitorial order, where citizens' fundamental right to privacy is breached by fellow citizens is destructive of social order. The notion of fundamental rights, such as a right to privacy as part of right to life, is not merely that the state is enjoined from derogating from them. It also includes the responsibility of the state to uphold them against the actions of others in the society, even in the context of exercise of fundamental rights by those others....

"...There is an inherent danger in making exceptions to fundamental principles and rights on the fly. Those exceptions, bit by bit, would then eviscerate the content of the main right itself. Undesirable lapses in upholding of fundamental rights by the legislature, or the executive, can be rectified by assertion of constitutional principles by this court.... We are not proposing that Constitutions cannot be interpreted in a manner that allows the nation-state to tackle the problems it faces. The principle is that exceptions cannot be carved out willy-nilly, and without forethought as to the damage they may cause."

To sum up, the right to privacy is like the elephant, easy to detect, yet all but impossible to define. Statutes do exist in Canada as well as in the U.S. But the experience is not particularly inspiring. The best course then is to give the strongest protection possible for the right to privacy in any statute that may be enacted

Right to Privacy vis-à-vis Right to Information

*"When it comes to privacy and accountability, people always demand the former for themselves and the latter for everyone else." – **David Brin***

The above state quotation is something that relates to this chapter. Privacy is something we all demand, no one is ready to divulge his personal information about anything, but when it come to a public figure, or a corporate entity or for that matter of fact any person who is in some way important to the society or remotely related to development of any part of the nation, every living soul wants to get information about their commercial; private; social affairs under the pretext of accountability or corporate social responsibility.

But what people forget is that the law is equal for everyone. The law cannot be used to compel a person to divulge certain information on request of another person, when the latter himself is not ready to be accountable.

In this chapter I will compare one of the two most contradicting rights; we have ever had in the Indian history. The Right to information as we all knows empowers us to know what was previously not allowed to.

When the act was passes, everyone thought it would bring about a revolution, but did it really help us? Or was it just another failed act of the government. The word 'right', it says 'you can ask for information from the authority', that is 'public authority' only. But apart from the 'public', there is also some 'private' information that we need to know. There lies the conflict, because no private individual or organization would be willing to disclose any vital private information to a no-man. The one thing which comes to fore of my mind when a person says to me, that he has the right to information, is that to what extent does the right to information empower a person to poke into someone's private affairs and does it at all give a right to any person to interfere in the affairs of a person on the pretext of the right to information act.

A Constitutional right cannot be legally denied by the government. On the other hand civil rights are the protections and privileges of personal liberty given to all citizens by law. Examples of civil rights and liberties include the right to get redressed if injured by another, right to privacy he right of peaceful protest, the right to a fair investigation and a trial if suspected of a crime, and more generally based. Constitutional rights such as the right to vote, the right to personal liberty, the right to life, the right to freedom of movement, the right to business and profession, the right to freedom of speech and expression. As the civilizations started to emerge and grow, these rights formalized through written Constitutions. Some of the more important civil rights were granted to citizens.

The term 'privacy' has been described[98] as "the rightful claim of the individual to determine the extent to which he wishes to share of himself with others and his control over the time, place and circumstances to communicate with others. It means the right to withdraw or to participate as he sees fit. It also means the individual's right to control dissemination of information about himself; it is his personal procession". Privacy has also been defined as a 'Zero-relationship' between two or more persons in the sense that there is no communication or interaction between them, if they so choose. Numerous legal and moral philosophers have suggested that privacy is valued because it satisfies a number of basic human needs. What is to be noted here is that, even information is also a kind of basic human need.[99]

What shall be done in a situation where one is keeping information just for the sake of keeping that information secret, and denies disclosing the information? The question that comes up is that the right to information act is equipped to handle such a situation and is it legit to interfere under such pretext? The line drawn between public and private is not so prominent right now. As long as the line remains faint, the question against RTI Act's powers will arise again and again.

---

[98] Global Media Journal – Indian Edition Winter Issue / December 2010 DOES RIGHT TO PRIVACY EXEMPT RIGHT TO KNOW? A CASE STUDY IN THE INDIAN CONTEXT

[99] http://www.caluniv.ac.in/global-mdia-journal/WINTER%20 2010%20STUDENTS'%20RESEARCH/Student%20 Research%202.pdf

I would discuss few cases which would make it clearer as to what I am trying to say here. To start with, we can have a look at the Singur issue. What happened there is history now. The TATA's (an Indian auto mobile company) were not allowed to set up a car factory in Singur[100] the TATAs were then asked to show how many acres of land were not used. But they blatantly refused to divulge any information stating that it was a deal signed by state government and the company. Disclosing a trade secret to a 'third party' may harm their trade interests.

An encroachment upon one's privacy is only shielded if the offender is the state and not a private entity. If the offender is a private individual then there is no effective remedy except in tort where one claims damages for intruding in his privacy and no more. In R. Rajagopal v State of Tamil Nadu[101] the Apex Court held that the right to privacy is a 'right to let alone'. No one can publish anything concerning the above matters without his consent, whether truthful or otherwise and whether laudatory or critical. If he does so, he would be violating the right to privacy of the person concerned and would be liable in the action of damages.

If we take into consideration the above mentioned cases amongst other such as the Kharak Singh judgment[102] I can definitely sense the contradiction of the right to know and the ways in which one can keep his secrets within him. The

---

[100]   a place near Hoogly district, West Bengal, was selected for auto mobile hub

[101]   Ibid

[102]   Discussed at length in earlier chapters

problem that some people feel while obtaining an answer to a RTI question is that the person/organization may simply say 'this is my right to privacy, I am not liable to answer these questions', and that ways there is no answer to the question raised. What needs to be analyzed here is that was the question relevant for just one person or for the entire public at large.

Illustratively, in the following instances, the CIC has denied requests for information on grounds of unwarranted intrusion of privacy: where call records of third parties were requested[103], copies of 'annual confidential reports' of other employees, bank statements of a partner of a firm[104], copy of a CBI charge sheet against an officer of an organization[105], details of all passengers who were on a particular flight[106], income tax returns of a third party[107], number of employees of an organization who had committed suicide[108] etc.

---

[103] Mr.S.Rajamohan v Bsnl, Chennai, (2009), CIC/AD/A/X/09/00129

[104] Ms. Kanchan Vora v Union Bank Of India, (2008), http://indiankanoon.org/doc/456808/

[105] Shri P. Thavasiraj v Dept. Of Atomic Energy, (2008), http://indiankanoon.org/doc/1718696/

[106] K.P. Subhashchandran v National Aviation Company, (2008), http://indiankanoon.org/doc/1067875/

[107] Mrs.Shobha R. Arora v. Income Tax (2006), Mumbai, Ms. Neeru Bajaj Vs. Income Tax (2007), Bimal Kanti Datta v Income Tax Department, (2008), http://indiankanoon.org/doc/292462/

[108] Shri.Chetan Kothari vs Bhabha Atomic Research Centre (2011), http://indiankanoon.org/doc/425930/

Ratan Tata, one of the industrialists whose conversation with Radia was published, has filed a case in the Delhi High Court seeking an injunction against the publication of these tapes on grounds of violation of his 'right to privacy'. This controversy has churned a debate on the conditions under which wiretapping may be lawfully conducted and the uses to which such information may be put. Although not the first instance of this kind, the controversy provides an immediate and emotive fulcrum to anchor discussion concerning issues of privacy and transparency that our study aims to raise

Tata holds that as Radia's phones were tapped by government agencies specially for investigating a possible offence, the recorded conversations should have been used for that purpose alone.

Ratan Tata has submitted his petition before Supreme Court asking to protect his right to privacy, for which he made the following requests:

i. "direct the ministry of home, finance, director general income tax and the CBI to take immediately retrieve and recover as far as possible all recordings that have been removed from their custody";

ii. "direct the government through the CBI or any other authority a thorough enquiry into the manner in which these secrets records were, contrary to the rules, made available and/or became available to those not authorized to so receive the recordings before this court";

iii. "direct the government to ensure that no further publication of these recordings, either as audio files through the Internet o has any print as transcripts appears in any media-print or electronic-and for that purpose take steps as may be necessary, ...under the Cable Television Networks Regulation Act, 1995, the Information Technology Act, 2000, the Information Technology Act, 2000, the Code of Criminal Procedure, 1973, read with the Indian Penal Code, 1860, and any other law as may be necessary." Chief of Tata group is begging for right to life, invoking Article 32 to secure Article 21. But given that freedom of information laws have at their core the purpose of disclosure, exemptions are strictly construed, and it has been said that the public right to know should prevail unless disclosure would publicize intimate details of a highly personal nature.

The Radia tapes so far published public issue, but not personal life of Tata. These conversations would be available to every citizen under the RTI Act because the only objection that one could raise would be on the ground of 8(j) of the RTI Act which says-information which relates to personal information, the disclosure of which has no relationship to any public activity or interest. It also says "or which would cause unwarranted invasion of the privacy of the individual unless the public authority is satisfied, unless the information officer is satisfied that the larger public interest justifies the disclosure of such an information."

In that case a preliminary question that should be asked is whether Tata's conversations would be revealed through an RTI, or whether his conversations would fall under the exemption of personal information found in section 8(j). It is interesting to note the structure of this exemption.

By the use of the word "or" the legislation suggests that unwarranted invasion of individual privacy may trigger the exemption, even if the information has a relationship to public activity or interest. But the added caveat says that the larger public interest could justify the release of even purely private information. In addition, what constitutes "personal" information has not been defined in the legislation.

In my opinion, the requests made by Mr. Ratan Tata seem legit to me, as what was caught while tapping Radia'a phone was for some other motive and not for incriminating or prosecuting everyone who was in touch or was an acquaintance. As the matter is still sub-judice I would refrain from commenting any further. However, there is something I would like to mention, and that is that the right to privacy is a greater right than the right to information if concealment of information is not in any way dangerous to the integrity, sovereignty and dignity of our nation and also the public at large doesn't suffer. This is to say that for greater good, private benefits shall always be overlooked.

In a **famous case** an applicant sought information from the Census Department on the 'religion and faith' of Sonia Gandhi – the President of the largest party currently in power in India. Both the Central Information Commission – the apex body adjudicating RTI appeals as well as the Punjab and Haryana High Court upheld the denial of information as it would otherwise lead to an unwarranted incursion into her privacy.[109]

In several cases, the CIC has astutely balanced the competing interests of transparency and privacy and has ordered disclosure where public interest was manifestly at issue. The CIC has ordered disclosure of a list of public servants being prosecuted for offences by the Central Vigilance Commission.[110]

It has ordered disclosure of details of the number of beneficiaries from a particular village under a loan scheme and amount disbursed by a public sector bank, whilst ordering the names of the beneficiaries to be withheld, students have been able to obtain copies of their mark sheets in public exams.

My only question here is, if a celebrity, a bolly-wood star can be asked to divulge information, then why couldn't the congress chief be? Was it right on the parts of authority to not to provide information. However, on the other hand religion and faith are overtly private matters of a an individual, and as Mahatma Gandhi said, that the function

---

[109] High Court dismisses appeal seeking information on Sonia Gandhi's religion, NDTV, November 29, 2010, http://www.ndtv.com/article/india/high-court-dismisses-appeal-seeking-information-on-sonia-gandhi-s-religion-69356

[110] Shruti Singh Chauhan v Directorate Of Vigilance, (2008), http://indiankanoon.org/doc/1128532/
Holding that "Information about alleged wrongdoing of Public servants,- verified by a process of investigation,- cannot be termed as private information which must be hidden from the Sovereign Masters of this democracy- the Citizens

of state is limited to fiscal, social and other aspects of life of an individual and does not extend to religious belief of the individual, the CIC was right in not giving out the information and it was able to act in accordance to the thin line that exists between right to privacy and right to information.

UID a Boon or a Sham- comparative
STUDY IN LIGHT OF RIGHT TO PRIVACY

The Unique Identity (hereinafter UID) project popularly known as Adhaar Card has been depicted to be a new face of development that technology could bring about. The UID project has also been sold to masses in India as a solution for accessibility to the service delivery, and as a tool for the eradication of ill-governance[111]. Though the UID tries to build up recognition and legitimacy on the basis of transparency, and delivery of good governance there are also issues of larger importance that have gone unnoticed by many. These include issues of the privacy and dignity of an individual being affected by the proposed UID scheme. An alarming fact is that little concern has been raised by opposition parties regarding the constitutionality and human rights implications that the UID scheme could cause. It is natural to have apprehensions and doubts about the effectiveness of implementation of the UID project, as this scheme is traversing through uncharted waters. Thus, it is important to analyze the socio-political implications in the context of the present political economy in India.

---

[111] Usha Ramanthan, A Unique Identity Bill, Economic and Political Weekly, 10-14 (2010).

The UID scheme could be viewed as an intended shift in relationship between the state, the market, and the citizen in the new age of globalization and technological advancement[112]. It is very important to note that by merely providing a UID number to an individual, there is no guarantee of developmental accessibility, or rights and benefits that would be accrued to the poor and marginalized communities in India. The National Identification Authority of India Bill, 2010, which has been mooted for the purpose of providing legal status to the UID project, has raised many concerns including, privacy issues, and mechanisms for effective service delivery. More over civil society has pointed out that the legislative and administrative mechanisms created by the UID authority have not been created through a consultative - democratic process.

Problems and Issues Posed by the UID Project

UID is a product of what started as an idea of biometric identity cards for the border Tates in India in the wake of the increased terrorist activity. In a report, the consulting agency that was meant to determine the feasibility of the biometric card for border communities suggested that the identity cards could be implemented to the entire country[113]. Now the government is trying to implement the new UID

---

[112] Ravi Shukla, Reimagining Citizenship: Debating India's Unique Identification Scheme, Economic and Political Weekly, 31-36 (2010)

[113] Sheetal Asrani-Dann, The Right to Privacy in the Era of Smart Governance: Concerns Raised By the Introduction of Biometric-Enabled National ID Cards in India, 47 The Journal of India Law Institute, 53-95 (2005)

scheme by masking it as a developmental agenda. Deeper questions of surveillance by the state, invasion of privacy at all levels, and the very fact of human beings being depicted to be mere numbers in the eyes of state leading to violation of dignity arise as a result of the UID project.

Issue of Surveillance by State

An important aspect that needs to be understood is that as of now, the various data that is collected is stored across multiple sources, and data required for a particular purpose is being taken from individuals at one time. This leads to the creation of informational silos[114]. For example, the data required for booking a rail ticket shall be different from that of opening a bank account. But now with UID, which aims to be used as a multipurpose identification system, all the data pertaining to an individual could be accessed at one time. This could lead to a situation where an individuals' autonomy, which is a well enshrined concept in human rights philosophy by the great philosophers such as Emanuel Kant[115], could be severely compromised. In other words, every decision made by a human in India could be under state surveillance. This could potentially lead to the denial of, and access to, many important social opportunities and other facilities for a particular section of people, who could be discriminated against by the state, using the information gathered from the UID. This has

---

[114] Supra n.1

[115] Immanuel Kant (Translated by Herbert James Paton) The moral law: groundwork of the metaphysic of morals, 42 (2005)

been referred to as "functional creep", which constitutes the expansion of the ambit of usage of a particular system from its initial limit.

UID in the post-9/11 scenario of 'state paranoidism' could lead to unwanted monitoring and surveillance by the state. One of the objectives claimed by the UID is that of assisting the state in national security.

But as mentioned above, the functional creep aspect may lead to the state monitoring at a level where an individual's decision making is negatively affected. The UID scheme could also lead to providing the state and intelligence agencies information to legitimate surveillance, but in doing so would infringe on individuals privacy[116].

It is evident that the UID scheme could lead to providing more power to the hands of the state, impact the lives of the citizen, and also may lead to the implementation of hidden agendas. We should not forget the fact that in the Rwandan genocide it was by using identity cards that the demarcation of the Tutsis and Hutus could be done.

Almost every country that tried to implement national identity cards based on integrated systems had public resistance, because of concerns over privacy. There are many dimensions to privacy viz. the privacy of a person, privacy of communications, territorial privacy and privacy of personal data.

Privacy of the person concerns the privacy of body, and its integrity and freedom of not being infringed upon.

---

[116] Shuddharbrata Sengupta, Every Day Surveillance in Sarai Reader 2002: The Cities of Everyday Life, 297-301 (2002)

Privacy of communications deals with the freedom to have communications by any means without being infringed upon by surveillance, telephone tapping etc.

Territorial privacy addresses freedom from encroachment into domestic and official spaces by the way of surveillance. Identity and informational privacy or data privacy deals with the protection of information, especially sensitive information.

It is important to note that the main privacy concerns brought by the UID project are: territorial and data privacy. In India, the concept of privacy in the social sphere is not as prevalent as it is in Europe or the United States.

A great observation made by Justice Brandeis and Samuel Warren in their article in Harvard Law review clearly shows the importance of limiting the impact and encroachment of technologies into the private sphere. Justice Brandeis observed that:

> "The intensity and complexity of life, attendant upon advancing civilization, have rendered necessary some retreat from the world, and man, under the refining influence of culture, has become more sensitive to publicity, so that solitude and privacy have become more essential to the individual; but modern enterprise and invention have, through invasions upon his privacy, subjected him to mental pain and distress, far greater than could be inflicted by mere bodily injury."[117]

---

[117] Samuel Warren and Louis D. Brandeis, The Right To Privacy, 4 Harvard Law Review 193 (1890)

The UID leads to a situation of access to all the sensitive information of the people enrolled in the UID. This information could be misused by authorities. The risk that the UID poses to an individual's privacy is enormous as information that is now scattered in the public domain will be brought into one point of convergence through the UID. Further, there are issues of privacy infringement due to the use of biometric information in the project. The collection of, and identification based on biometric information could be understood as a breach of one's territorial privacy and one's data privacy.

As persons are being identified on the basis of sensitive biometric information, the risk of being profiled, targeted and marginalized by the state on the basis of this sensitive information is very high. Hence, there is a requirement for the protection of data privacy and territorial privacy. The claims that the UID number will provide efficient access to developmental projects and facilities, should be viewed with suspicion, because when sensitive information of this nature is placed in the control of the state, it gives enormous power to the state.

Tackling the Issues Arising Out of the UID

After having discussed the issues above, it is now necessary to chalk out ways to reconcile the differences between the right to privacy under the Constitution of India and the UID and ways to approach the issues arising out of The National Identification Authority of India Bill, 2010.

Regarding the right to privacy in India, the decisional jurisprudence has clearly acknowledged the fact that it forms part of Article 21. In this context privacy can be understood as the right to be left alone, as envisaged by the Justice Louis Brandeis. Being a right, that is acknowledged to be part of Article 21; violation of this right by the proposed UID scheme would seem to be unconstitutional.

When considering this, one aspect that needs to be kept in mind is that the cases that have come before the Supreme Court have thus far been related to the privacy of a person and privacy of communications. There have been no affirmative rulings of the right to privacy in any cases regarding personal data and territorial privacy. Also legislations such as the Anti-Terrorism Act of 2002, Information Technology Act of 2000 and the Telegraph Act of 1885 have limited restriction on privacy.

Privacy in our country is not a right that is clearly stated; therefore clarity is important as projects such as the UID are increasing the need for individuals to have the right to privacy. Also, there is a need for a comprehensive privacy legislation, which would ensure the protection of personal and sensitive data, and which may also establish a regulatory body. Perhaps such privacy legislation could be structured along similar lines as the data protection commissioner's offices, which exist in Canada, Ireland and other developed informational economies.

Tackling the Issues Arising Out of the UID

After having discussed the issues above, it is now necessary to chalk out ways to reconcile the differences between the right to privacy under the Constitution of India and the UID and ways to approach the issues arising out of The National Identification Authority of India Bill, 2010.

Regarding the right to privacy in India, the decisional jurisprudence has clearly acknowledged the fact that it forms part of Article 21. In this context privacy can be understood as the right to be left alone, as envisaged by the Justice Louis Brandeis. Being a right, that is acknowledged to be part of Article 21; violation of this right by the proposed UID scheme would seem to be unconstitutional.

When considering this, one aspect that needs to be kept in mind is that the cases that have come before the Supreme Court have thus far been related to the privacy of a person and privacy of communications. There have been no affirmative rulings of the right to privacy in any cases regarding personal data and territorial privacy. Also legislations such as the Anti-Terrorism Act of 2002, Information Technology Act of 2000 and the Telegraph Act of 1885 have limited restriction on privacy.

Privacy in our country is not a right that is clearly stated; therefore clarity is important as projects such as the UID are increasing the need for individuals to have the right to privacy. Also, there is a need for a comprehensive privacy legislation, which would ensure the protection of personal and sensitive data, and which may also establish a regulatory body. Perhaps such privacy legislation could be structured along similar lines as the data protection commissioner's offices, which exist in Canada, Ireland and other developed informational economies.

Further it is also important to highlight the fact that The National Identification Authority of India Bill, 2010[118] completely ignores the issue of privacy. Within the Bill there exist no provisions that would help in the protection of an individual's personal privacy. Further, there is a great amount of brouhaha around Clause 33 of the proposed Bill. Clause 33 states that the disclosure of information for national security, which runs the risk of surveillance, tracking, profiling and social, shall be controlled by the state and its agents.

The Bill does not make the UID a mandatory requirement - as per the Clause 3 - it is the option of the individual to choose if he/she wants the UID. Hence the Authority claims that there is no breach of privacy as the people have consented, and have voluntarily provided their information. But there are two aspects that must be considered. One is that even though there is no explicit compulsion for a person to obtain a UID number, there may be indirect compulsion, due to exclusion and inaccessibility to services and facilities for those who do not have a UID number. Thus, in this sense the UID number will become mandatory. The second point to consider is that even though the information is given voluntarily, the right to privacy over sensitive personal information does not exist. To avoid

---

[118]   The draft bill of bill- http://www.psrindia.org/uploads/media//NIA%20Draft%20Bill.pdf.

situations where an individual's privacy is violated by the UID scheme, there needs to be both a specific provision that states clearly that no particular services or facilities shall be denied to citizen on basis of lack of UID, and a provision protecting the privacy of collected information.

In my opinion, the UID scheme is a failure to the extent that sensitive personal information may be leaked and that will be a cause of grave concern, as it might lead to increase in white-collar crimes, identity thefts, and fiscal crimes of a different nature. It may also lead to invasion of privacy and may lower the dignity of the person whose information is leaked.

Therefore this scheme needs to be scrutinized carefully and a constant vigilance is required over the operating of the system prescribed under the scheme.

This picture clearly lays down the negatives of the UID scheme. So in my opinion the UID scheme is a sham and not a boon.

Advancement in Technology and its Relevance to Right to Privacy

With the advancement in technology and emerging computer and communications techniques have radically altered the ways in which we communicate and exchange information.

Along with the speed, efficiency, and cost-saving benefits of the digital revolution come new challenges to the security and privacy of communications and information traversing the global communications infrastructure. In response to these challenges, the security mechanisms of traditional paper-based communications media envelopes and locked filing cabinets are being replaced by cryptographic security techniques. Through the use of cryptography, communication and information stored and transmitted by computers can be protected against interception to a very high degree. The law on privacy has not kept pace with technological development.

Advances in computer technology and telecom-munications have dramatically increased the amount of information that can be stored, retrieved, accessed and collated almost instantaneously. An enormous amount of personal information is held by various bodies, both public and private - the police, the income tax department, banks, insurance agencies, credit-rating agencies, stockbrokers, employers, doctors, lawyers, marriage bureaus, detectives, airlines, hotels and so on. Till recently, this information was held on paper; the sheer Vol. and a lack of centralization made it hard to collate with the result that it was very difficult for one body or person to use this information effectively. In the Internet age, information is so centralized and so easily accessible that one tap on a button could throw up startling amounts of information about an individual. This enables public authorities to keep a closer watch over the individual.

It doesn't end with public authorities. There are other Big Brothers watching everywhere. Every time you log on to the Internet you leave behind an electronic trail. Websites and advertising companies are able to track users as they travel on the Internet to assess their personal preferences, habits and lifestyles. This information is used for direct marketing campaigns that target the individual customer. Every time you use your credit card you leave behind a trail of where you shopped and when, what you bought, your brand preferences, your favorite restaurant.

In this electronic environment, the need for privacy-enhancing technologies is apparent.

Communications applications such as electronic mail and electronic fund transfers require secure means of encryption and authentication features that can only be provided if cryptographic knowhow is widely available and unencumbered by government regulation. Governmental regulation of cryptographic security techniques endangers personal privacy[119]. Encryption ensures the confidentiality of personal records, such as medical information, personal financial data, and electronic mail.

Advantages of Encryption

The various advantages of encryption are:[120]

1. Encryption can protect information stored on the computer from unauthorized access even from people who otherwise have access to your computer system.

2. Encryption can protect information while it is in transit from one computer system to another.

3. Encryption can be used to verify another of a document.

4. Encryption can be used to deter and detect accidental or international alteration in data.

One sad incident that I would like to put in here is the infamous DPS DELHI MMS SCANDAL, which invaded the privacy of two people due to advancement in technology and let to dire consequences.

---

[119] Theodore F. Claypoole:- "Privacy Regulations a Concern with Internet" LexisNexis Martindale-Hubbell (R) Legal Articles

[120] Anoop MS (2007). Public key Cryptography - Applications Algorithms and Mathematical Explanations. India: Tata Elxsi. P.67-68

BRIEF REVIEW OF THE FACTS OF THE CASE

The story started when a sexually explicit video clip of two school students was shot with a cell phone camera and then distributed among friends through the Multimedia Messaging Service (MMS). The clip, showing a young girl engaged in oral sex with a boy, was shot with her consent but was circulated to the others without her permission. The clip then landed in the hands of a smart entrepreneur who tried to make easy money out of it. Mr. Ravi Raj, a final year M.Sc. Geophysics student of Indian Institute of Technology, Kharagpur had opened an account under the name 'Alice Electronics' on the auction site *Bazee.com* on 21'st of July, 2004. He posted the clip in that account on the 27'th of November, 2004 under the header 'DPS Girl having fun' and it remained there till 29'th November, 2004. Mr. Raj was arrested on 14'th December and produced before a Delhi court two days later. The Court remanded him to three days police custody. Meanwhile, the CEO of Bazee. com, Mr. Avnish Bajaj, was sentenced to jail for six days by a Delhi court. Mr. Bajaj sought his release on bail on the ground that he had been co-operating with the police in the investigation of the case and had flown in from Mumbai to assist the probe. He was granted bail later. The DPS boy who was at the centre of the MMS controversy was also arrested and bought before a Juvenile Court in Delhi. Describing the alleged act as a 'misadventure' and not 'moral depravation', The Principal Magistrate of Juvenile Justice Board granted him bail. On December 24, 2004 the other accused Mr. Ravi Raj was also granted bail by a Delhi court considering the fact that the prime accused have already been released on bail.

The impact of the incident was that the Delhi government by its notification dated February 1, 2005 banned the use of mobile phones not only by students but also by teachers in all government-run or aided schools. The most ironical part of the story is that it concluded without even knowing what the female student visible in the clip had to say or confess.

THE ARGUMENTS

While all this self-righteous rhetoric is fine and dandy, it doesn't take us anywhere. So, let us proceed to the arguments, one by one: Firstly: The porn clip was posted on the Bazee site only after the 'poster' i.e. Mr. Ravi Raj clicked 'Agree' on the Terms and Conditions of the Bazee site which explicitly prohibited the posting of pornographic materials. This means that what happened was against the rules of Bazee.com.

Now, one may argue that it was Bazee.com's responsibility to filter material posted on the website. It could have been done automatically as well. But a computer, by its very nature is incapable of interpreting information. There is no computer in existence which can open a video clip and examine the data because a computer cannot be programmed to understand video data. In fact, Bazee does have existing processes and safeguards to ensure that it provides a trustworthy and safe marketplace for the community. These include a 'system scan' for banned/ suspect key words. But it is only capable of scanning the text heading under which the message was posted. Now, in this case the header was 'DPS Girl having fun', which as a popular newspaper pointed out is something any normal internet savvy person would instantly identify as porn. But the filtering program unsurprisingly found nothing wrong with it because there is nothing objectionable in the words 'DPS', 'girl', 'having' and 'fun'.

Besides this, there is also a 'community watch' whereby users can alert them as to the listings that are potentially in violation of the user agreement. Items listed on the site and found to be in infringement of the user agreement are removed from the site immediately and the sellers may be subject to suspension.

Section 67 of the Act states that: 'whoever publishes or transmits or causes to be published in the electronic form, any material which is lascivious or appeals to the prurient interest or if its effect is such as to tend to deprave and corrupt persons who are likely, having regard to all relevant circumstances, to read, see or hear the matter contained or embodied in it, shall be punished on first conviction with imprisonment of either description for a term which may extend to five years and with fine which may extend to one lakh rupees and in event of a second or subsequent conviction with imprisonment of either description for a term which may extend to ten years and also with fine which may extend to two lakh rupees.' As far as the CEO of Bazee. com is concerned, he is not even tangentially involved in the publication or transmission of the obscene video clip. The question is can you blame the CEO of an auction site for providing a platform to lead this 'viral' attack? Going by the same logic, why should we spare the mobile operators, who provide the MMS (or SMS) platform for the spread of porn?

ANALYSIS

This incident involves two aspects; one is the control of sexuality and the other control of technology. The point at which both these anxieties of control — of sex and of technology — converge is pornography.

This clip was a private affair of two individuals, however due to inappropriate conduct on part of those involved in circulating this clip, made the issue media sensitive and led to grave invasion into the privacy of the victim of the clip.

Owing to their diverse character, there are many difficulties in protecting the unique features of the Internet and Computers within the existing framework of the legal regime of intellectual property laws. The framework of the Intellectual Property statutes is not sufficient to cover the new aspects of Information Technology. Due to this insufficiency, Courts often have to rely on their own interpretations of existing statutes to make them applicable to such disputes. Moreover, due to global connectivity it becomes very difficult to search for liability and establish jurisdiction over/upon the entity responsible for the crime.

The cyber laws were formed years back when the technology of camera phones did not exist in India. The laws do not deal at length with issues such as cyber defamation, cyber harassment, cyber nuisance etc., which are required to be looked upon as soon as possible. Even the Information Technology Act, 2000 does not have any provisions to prevent pornography via the medium of cell phones.

Monitoring of voice and other data flowing through telecom network is also not a plausible solution to the problems highlighted by the 'MMS scandal'. No customer would want its conversations, messages, and pictures to be monitored by the telecom network as it would amount to breach of privacy

The only way out is better societal discipline, mobile etiquette as well as up-to-date cyber laws. Another suggestive measure could be formulation of equipment manufacturer's law, mandating the cell phone manufacturers to include additional technology of a sound beep, audible at the range of 10 feet, when a picture is being clicked. This would forewarn the person being photographed. This law was enacted just days back in South Korea for dealing with mobile-related crimes.

Section 72 of the Act, establishing an Information Technology Offence of "Breach of Confidentiality and Privacy" reads as under:

> *"72. Breath of confidentiality and privacy.—Save as otherwise provided in this Act or any other law for the time being in force, if any person who, in pursuance of any of the powers conferred under this Act, rules or regulations made there under, has secured access to any electronic record, book, register, correspondence, information, document or other material without the consent of the person concerned discloses such electronic record, book, register, correspondence, information, document or other material to any other person shall be punished with imprisonment for a term which may extend to two years, or with fine which may extend to one lakh rupees, or with both."*

It will be noted that this provision deals only with information collected by a person who secures the information in pursuance of powers that he or she exercises under the Act. It punishes with imprisonment or fine or both the disclosure of such information to third parties without the consent of the person who the information relates to. This provision would, therefore, be extremely narrow in its application, being relevant only to offences by authorities such as Adjudicating Officers, the members of the CRAT or Certifying Authorities under the Act.

Employee privacy is under siege: employers routinely use software to access their employees' email and every move of the employee at the workplace and this is in turn an invasion in to privacy.

Field sales representatives have their movements tracked by the use of location-based tracking systems in new wireless phones.

Technology blurs the traditional boundaries between systems. Techniques such as data mining ensure that every bit of valuable information is extracted and logged. Data matching enables linkages to be made between the contents of previously uncorrelated databanks.

It is apparent that the larger issue of online privacy has remained completely outside the scope of the legislation. There seems to be no particular authority concerned with understanding the importance of the issue and bringing in regulations to curb unscrupulous use of personal information. It is not even as if a self-regulatory model for online business is in place and legislation is not required. It is important that legislators understand that the protection of personally identifiable information is vital if one seeks to foster a secure and trustworthy electronic environment the avowed purpose of the IT Act. This is one void in law and policy that just cannot be ignored.

MEDIA AND THE RIGHT TO PRIVACY

The development of the media in modern times has a special relevance to the evolution of the law of privacy. The media has made it possible to bring the private life of an individual into the public domain, thus exposing him to the risk of an invasion of his space and his privacy. At a time when information was not so easily accessible to the public, the risk of such an invasion was relatively remote. In India, newspapers were, for many years, the primary source of information to the public. Even they had a relatively limited impact, given that the vast majority of our population was illiterate. This has changed with a growth in public consciousness, a rise in literacy and perhaps most importantly, an explosion of visual and electronic media which have facilitated an unprecedented information revolution.

With the advent in media and its technology, invasion of privacy of people at large, especially public- figures, politicians, celebrities has increased rapidly. The media constantly exposes felonious acts in the society through Sting Operations. But, at the same time this is called violation of a major Human Right by media, i.e., Right to Privacy, as in some way they intrude the privacy of a person. Privacy is what is demanded by and for each and every person in his or her life, this privacy literary means nothing but being aloof from society on some issues of personal life. But, the question is, can Sting Operation, known as '*Dansh Patrakarita*' in Hindi, can take away this privacy and make it public. This is the most burning issue in the entire world today.

Article 12 of Universal Declaration of Human Rights (1948) defines Right to Privacy as:

"No one shall be subjected to arbitrary interference with his privacy, family, home or correspondence not to attack upon his honour and reputation. Everyone has the right to protection of law against such interference or attack."

The press has been guaranteed freedom under article 19 of the Indian Constitution but till what extent does this freedom extends, is still to be ascertained.

Romesh Thapar Case[121] the Supreme Court laid down an important principle and giving restrictive interference to clause 2 of Article 19 having allowed the imposition of restrictions on the freedom of speech and expression for specified purposes, any law imposing restriction which are capable of being applied in causes beyond the express purposes cannot be held to be constitutional or valid to any extent.

On the other hand, '*Freedom of Press*' has been held to be a part of the Fundamental Right of '*Freedom of Speech and expression*' guaranteed by article 19(1)(a) to the citizens of India. Is had been held that '*Freedom of Press*' is necessary

---

[121]   AIR 1950 S.C. 124

for exercise of fundamental freedom of citizens of 'speech and expression'.[122] And so *'Freedom of Press'* cannot be termed as unconstitutional and void. And as the Constitution says this can only be exercised till it does not harm the decency/morality of a person. The Constitution of India gives full liberty to press but with strings attached, on 18th June, 1951 Amended Article 19(2) by adding "*reasonable*" to restrictions. The restriction must be reasonable. In other words, it must not be excessive or misappropriate. The procedure and the manner of imposition of the restriction also must be just, fair and reasonable.

In a landmark judgment in the case of **Sakal papers**,[123] the Supreme Court held that Article 19(2) of the Constitution permits imposition of reasonable restrictions on the heads specified in Article 19(2) and on no other grounds. It is, therefore, not open for the state to curtail the *Freedom of Speech and Expression* for promoting the general welfare of a section or a group of people unless its action can be justified by the law falling under clause 2 of Article 19. And moreover it is valid point that at a certain point all Sting Operations do violate *Right to Privacy* in some degree because during a Sting Operation, in nearly all its cases, the person being filmed is not aware of the presence of a hidden camera. This means that he does not consent to be filmed, without which, in ordinary course, no one has the right to film anyone. However, it may be argued that a illegal act being committed by a public servant during his office hours and in abuse of spirit of his office are not worthy of protection under Right to Privacy law. Besides, what a public servant

---

[122] *Hamdard Dawakhana v. Union of India*, AIR 1960 S.C. 554
[123] AIR 1962 S.C. 305

does while discharging his duty is in public domain. In such cases, public interest does seem to weigh heavier compared to *Right to Privacy*. If a person has no duty towards general public, his morality questionable conduct is not open to public scrutiny unless he violates the law by such conduct.

Sting Operations are generally carried out to trap the corrupt, the underworld dons and spies. They are also undertaken to establish adultery. Sting Operation can also be useful in the arrest of terrorists and anti-national elements. The spy camera of media caught 11 M.L.A.s accepting bribe for asking question in the parliament. When the media gets all the evidence against the corrupt and the wrongdoer and their aim is public interest, why do media not file a case in court and submit these as proof? This will lead to punishing of these wrongdoers, which is in public interest. Or, even after getting such evidences, why no report is given to public authorities and make them take some actions? By interviewing Mr. Prakash Tiwari, Bureau chief, Sahara Samaya, Bhopal, and Mr. Brajesh, a correspondent of Star News, Bhopal and Mr. Rajendra, a correspondent of Zee News, Bhopal it was found that Sting Operations are a good way to get evidences for exposing things and submitting these in court. It is a way of helping law, as media is the fourth estate of governance.

On 30 August, 2007 Live India, a news channel conducted a sting operation on a Delhi government school teacher forcing a girl student into prostitution. Subsequent to the media exposé, the teacher **Uma Khurana**[124] was

---

[124]   WP(Crl.) No.1175/2007

attacked by a mob and was suspended by the Directorate of Education, Government of Delhi. Later investigation and reports by the media exposed that there was no truth to the sting operation. The girl student who was allegedly being forced into prostitution was a journalist. The sting operation was a stage managed operation. The police found no evidence against the teacher to support allegations made by the sting operation of child prostitution. In this case, the High Court of Delhi charged the journalist with impersonation, criminal conspiracy and creating false evidence. The Ministry of Information and Broadcasting sent a show-cause notice to TV-Live India, alleging the telecast of the sting operation by channel was "defamatory, deliberate, containing false and suggestive innuendos and half truths."

Section 5 of the Cable Television Networks (Regulation) Act, 1995 and the Cable Television Network Rules (hereafter the Cable Television Networks Act), stipulates that no programme can be transmitted or retransmitted on any cable service which contains anything obscene, defamatory, deliberate, false and suggestive innuendos and half truths. The Rules prescribes a programming code to be followed by channels responsible for transmission/re-transmission of any programme.

The programme code restricts airing of programmes that offend decency or good taste, incite violence, contains anything obscene, defamatory, deliberate, false and suggestive innuendos and half truths, criticizes, maligns or slanders any individual in person or certain groups, segments of social, public and moral life of the country and affects the integrity of India, the President and the judiciary.

The programme code provided by the Rules is exhaustive. The Act empowers the government to restrict operation of any cable network it thinks is necessary or expedient to do so in public interest.

The court observed that false and fabricated sting operations violate a person's right to privacy. It further, observed, "Giving inducement to a person to commit an offence, which he is otherwise not likely and inclined to commit, so as to make the same part of the sting operation is deplorable and must be deprecated by all concerned including the media." It commented that while "…sting operations showing acts and facts as they are truly and actually happening may be necessary in public interest and as a tool for justice, but a hidden camera cannot be allowed to depict something which is not true, correct and is not happening but has happened because of inducement by entrapping a person."[125]

Freedom of Press is derived from the Freedom of Right to Speech and Expression guaranteed in article 19(1) (a) of the Constitution of India. Moreover, Right to Privacy flows from Right to Life and Personal Liberty guaranteed in article 21 of the Constitution of India. Both these come under Part III of the Constitution, i.e., the Fundamental Rights. So there is a clash in two major Fundamental Rights guaranteed by the Constitution of India. These Fundamental Rights are not absolute and can only be taken away in accordance to Article 19(2) under the pretext of reasonable restrictions.[126]

---

[125]   Ibid.

[126]   Hamdard Dawakhana v. Union of India, AIR 1960 S.C. 554

Abhishek Manu Singhvi wants to be forgotten, but not in the way his party is forgetting him, by removing this articulate Cantabrigian from its list of people entrusted to talk to the electronic media. The board bearing his name as the top-honcho in the party's human rights and legal affairs department has been removed. All this is quite ironic for I suspect that his sense of belonging and yearning to be accepted in the party has never been stronger than it is now.

Garnering spotlight he just did not want. Few people would want that the public be able to freely access a video that allegedly shows one in a sexual encounter. Just when the dust had somewhat settled, the effective blocking and removal of the 'offending' content has affecting the TRP ratings of the grainy Internet video. The elite-media has closed ranks for reasons both legal and fraternal and has let the video disappear from public memory. Of course the digital divide helps, given that the primary (if not the only) form in which this voyeuristic material was available was online – thus keeping out the rabble. The otherwise vociferous Indira Congress spokesperson remains muted at present, and possibly for the intermediate future. Lesser mortals will never know when exactly will poor Abhishek Manu be rehabilitated, what forces will line up to make it happen, how these forces make a call on a thing like this. It is sad that we will never know – it is sad because precisely these forces also make calls on public affairs too, hush up issues more embarrassing – like the nakedness of those who cannot afford basic clothing.

Lesser mortals are lesser in many other ways. Rare are the moments when people of stature appeal to 'everyone' opting for the humble 'we' to refer to all of us, addressing us, as if we are one community! In a well-articulated statement that essentially said nothing, Abhishek Manu Singhvi did however mention something interesting. In a half-philosophical tone, he called upon society to ponder upon the destabilizing consequences of extreme invasion of privacy in these times, done with technology that any small-town in India already has. He said "promoting or participating in a person's natural and understandable discomfiture, we must respect privacy issues. Hear, hear.

It is a case of the denizens of the fortress calling upon the impoverished city around it, to rise to some idea of 'common citizenship', when the chips are down. This statement, almost comically Niemolleresque in spirit, in a strange way underlines the apartheid society that exists in Lutyen's and South Delhi, engaging in motions and rituals of respecting privacies, oblivious to this vast and hard land. In Bangla, there is a common proverb – "haati kadaye porle byangeo laathi mare" – "when the elephant gets stuck in mud, even the lowly frog does not miss a chance to kick the giant." This urge to kick comes from soured dreams, from being the spectator of gold-adorned elephant processions for decades.

In these rare moments, doctored or not, the esteemed become human, like the rest of us. The non-urban swathes of the Indian Union are being disemboweled daily. Almost like vomit from mangled bowels, people end up in the cities, in splatters and streams, providing endless live footage of the kind no court order can restrict. The million honeymoons on dusty concrete is not a number. It is not even news in a country where an Indian diplomat's daughter's 48-hour detention in a New York City police station churned the collective sentiment of those who watch the gory roadside spectacle every day, could careless about the million plus women dehumanized in Indian jails, are mute about the rape and murder of 'anti-national' Manorama and think domestic-workers asking for two hundred rupees more are a nuisance.

I support Abhishek Manu Singhvi's right to privacy, not to be harassed, intruded and violated in full public view, even if notionally or in a doctored footage. No one deserves to be dehumanized like that. Media should realize its boundaries even when dealing with such figures. Even if what Manu Singhvi allegedly did, the purpose behind it being unethical, still he should have been accorded right to privacy to the extent that the lady involved shall be protected so as to safeguard her dignity and self respect in the eyes of her family and society at large.

The fact that the tape was proved fabricated does not undo the harm done to the people involved in it. This leads to burning debate between the two major Fundamental Rights which the makers of Constitution would never have thought of.

Freedom of press is important in a country like India, but reasonable restrictions are required to be put on every right and freedom of press is no exception. The press cannot interfere into the lives of any public figure without any reasonable cause. This phenomenon needs to be adhered to.

ANALYSIS OF THE PRIVACY BILL
AND SUGGESTIONS THEREOF

Right to Privacy is a very important Human Right. For long India ignored this important Civil Liberty despite demands for the same. Finally, Supreme Court of India interpreted Article 21 of the Constitution of India as a "Constitutional Source" of Right to Privacy in India.

The Personal Data Protection Bill 2006 was a simple 14 section bill. It said that "Personal Data" as defined shall not be collected without "Consent", shall not be disclosed for the purposes of "Direct marketing" or "Commercial Gain". Power to further legislate was left to the Central and State Governments with the proviso that there could be up to three Data Controllers for each State. Exemptions were given for detection of crime, prosecution of offenders or for collection of tax. Reporting to the Data Controller and mandating security and minimum collection principles were also indicated. Three year imprisonment and Rs 10 lakh fine was prescribed for violation along with compensation payable to the victim. Vicarious liability of corporate personnel was also included. Summary trial under CrPC was recommended for grievance Redressal. However the Bill was not passed and lapsed when the tenure of the previous Parliament ended. The Information Technology

Amendment Bill was however passed and became law as Information Technology Amendment Act 2008. (ITA 2008).

Now Right to Privacy is a Fundamental Right in India. However, exercise of a Fundamental Rights is very difficult in India without a support of a "Statutory Right" in this regard. This is the reason why we need to enact a Statutory Law on Right to Privacy in India.

Essential Features of a Good Privacy Legislation:

- Providing an enforceable Right to the Citizen;

- Establishing an effective monitoring mechanism;

- Imposing responsibilities on the data processor;

- Defining a noncompliance deterrence structure;

- Providing a Grievance Redressal mechanism;

- Avoid/Minimize overlapping of provisions with other legislations

Providing an Enforceable Right to the Citizen the most important aspect that we look for in the legislation is what the Right that is protected is and whether it is defined properly.

The **PB 2011 states under Section 3** that "All citizens shall have a right to privacy which shall not be infringed except in accordance with law and subject to provisions of this Act"

This states that there shall be a right to privacy but privacy itself is defined only through the definition of what constitutes "Infringements". The Privacy right is created by this law by defining the circumstances under which the right to privacy can be infringed. For all practical purposes, in future, this law will prevail over everything else including the interpretations of the Constitution when there was no such law.

The first observation on the Bill is therefore a thought that It would have been more effective if the "Right to Privacy" could have been derived and extended from the Constitution and the Privacy Bill focused only to set up an infrastructure to implement the constitutional guaranteed right and provide such clarifications as are necessary for the implementation.

By attempting to define the Right to Privacy by law we may be imposing restrictions on an extended interpretation of the "Right to Privacy". What the current approach has done is to define the "Right to Privacy" by the set of exclusions mentioned in the Bill which relate to how the data related to the person should or should not be handled. "Privacy Protection" under the Bill therefore does not go much beyond "Data Protection".

Under Section 5, four specific types of infringements are defined. Accordingly, the following activities shall be construed as infringements if they are undertaken in a manner not specifically authorized in the Act:

i. Collection, processing, storage and disclosure of Personal Data;

ii. Interception or monitoring of communications sent from or to the individual;

iii. Surveillance of the individual;

iv. Sending unsolicited commercial communications to the individual;

v. Section 4 and 6 indicate "When the Privacy Right can be infringed".

Under Section 4, it does not constitute infringement if privacy Rights are breached under the following circumstances.

1. sovereignty, integrity and security of India, strategic, scientific or economic interest of the State;

2. Preventing incitement to the commission of any offence;

3. Prevention of public disorder or detection of crime;

4. Protection of rights and freedoms of others;

5. In the interest of friendly relations with foreign states

Under these exemptions the provision on "Protection of rights and freedoms of others" is vague. It is perhaps meant the "Right to Freedom of Expression" and "Right to Information". It is better if the intention is clarified as otherwise such vague provisions are liable to be misused. Even "Preventing incitement" is too vague and is most likely to be misused. "Prevention of public order" can be extended to all cases of politically motivated issues and is another source of misuse. "Security of India" used in the first sub clause would have covered the cases of offence or crime and hence points 2 and 3 above can be deleted while point 4 could be made more specific.

Under Section 6, Publication by any mode for journalistic purpose is also exempt from Privacy unless it is proven that such publishing is of material which is reasonably expected to be held private. This perhaps can be identified with "Freedom of Press".

The rights specified above apply to "Personal Information" which is a very broad set of information about any living individual that is capable of individually identifying the person.

If the "Privacy Right" has to be taken beyond "Data Protection", it is necessary to define "Privacy" as a "Sense of personal liberty felt by an individual without the constraints felt by him as radiated by people around him".

The availability and disclosure of data about an individual to the people around is the prime reason for these constraints to be felt by the individual. Hence one of the concepts of Privacy is to give the right to the individual to control how much of the information about himself he would try to share with others. Under such a definition, data disclosure becomes a means of eroding the sense of privacy and therefore becomes part of the privacy protection mechanism.

This should then be addressed under three classifications namely, "Personal Data, "Sensitive Personal Data" and "Essential Data".

Essential data is one which the society has the right to know. It includes data on communicable diseases carried by the person etc which has a direct impact on the society.

Sensitive personal data is the data which the individual has absolute right to keep confidential like the one which a person would like to keep in his private diary. Personal data is the residual data about the person which includes his basic identity.

REMEDIES UNDER THE BILL

The Bill recognizes the right to privacy, in its various ambits. Hence, it also provides what all can be pursued in case of its violation. The following remedies are available to an aggrieved person:

- *Compensation*

Any person who suffers damage can claim for compensation any damage caused to him by any data controller, under section 76. The damage must be due to any contravention on part of the data controller. Here it is sought to be clarified that the amounts described in the table are with respect of penalties. These penalties operate as fines. They are intended to deter illegal conduct. However, compensation which is provided under Sec. 76 acts as a remedy aims to restitute the loss of the person complaining of damage.

- *Civil Remedies*

Section 84 provides that the individual, whose right to privacy has been adversely affected, may bring a civil action against such persons have caused such violation. This is addition to any criminal proceedings existing against such person (violator).

- *Criminal Remedies*

XIV provides for various offences that may be committed under the nature of right provided for under this bill. But, the rider is provided for under Section 82, where any Court may take cognizance of offence under this Bill, solely on the compliant made by the Authority.

Overlapping legislations

It is preferable if the overlapping of different legislations is minimized. The Bill envisages legislation on interception, surveillance, unsolicited communication etc. which overlap with ITA 2008 and Indian Telegraph Acts in particular.

It is better for the Government to consolidate the "Interception" related legislation in one Act applicable to all types of data under transit or storage. If necessary, such consolidation can be made under Privacy bill and the conflicting provisions removed from ITA 2008 and Indian

Telegraph Act. Alternatively one single authority to deal with "Interception" can be created under a new Act such as "Data Interception Act" which can address the issue in its entirety. Though this could mean rearrangement of administrative powers of different departments, it would work better in the long run.

CONCLUSION

I feel that the privacy legislations in India are still at infant stage, a lot needs to be done to make the legislations practical according to the present scenario.

Law is a living process, which changes according to the changes in society, science, and ethics and so on. Law is not static but it is dynamic. The legal system should imbibe developments and advances that take place in science as long as they do not violate fundamental legal principles and are for the good of the society.

The right to privacy in India has failed to acquire the status of an absolute right. The right in comparison to other competing rights, like, the right to freedom of speech & expression, the right of the State to impose restrictions on account of safety and security of the State, and the right to information, is easily relinquished. The exceptions to the right to privacy, such as, overriding public interest, safety and security of the State, apply in most countries. Nonetheless, as the book demonstrates, unwarranted invasion of privacy is widespread.

The right to privacy has not been explicitly granted by our Constitution even though it has been demanded by many quarters but implicitly it has been accepted as a natural individual right implied under Article 21 under the 'right to life' and this stands further vindicated by various court rulings.

The instance of privacy during the Mahabharata and Ramayana period is something which needed to be explained in order to understand how it evolved in India and its relevance to the Indian society.

For instance, in the UK, Sweden, France and Netherlands, the right to photograph a person or retouching of any picture is prohibited unlike, in India where press photographers do not expressly seek consent of the person being photographed, if he/she is in a public space. In France, not only is the publication of information is prohibited on account of the right to privacy, but the method in which the information is procured also falls within the purview of the right to privacy and could be violative. This includes information or photograph taken in both public and private spaces. Privacy within public spaces is recognized, especially, "where there is reasonable expectation of privacy." The Indian norms or code of ethics in journalism fail to make such a distinction between public and private space. Nor do the guidelines impose any restrictions on photographing an individual without seeking express consent of the individual.

The Indian media violates privacy in day-to-day reporting, like overlooking the issue of privacy to satisfy morbid curiosity. The PCI norms prohibit such reporting, unless it is outweighed by 'genuine overriding public interest'. Almost all the above countries prohibit publication of details that would hurt the feelings of the victim or his/her family. Unlike the UK, where the PCC can pass desist orders, in India the family and/or relatives of the victims are hounded by the media.

In India, the right to privacy is not a positive right. It comes into effect only in the event of a violation. The law on privacy in India has primarily evolved through judicial intervention. It has failed to keep pace with the technological advancement and the burgeoning of the 24/7 media news channels. The prevalent right to privacy is easily compromised for other competing rights of 'public good', 'public interest' and 'State security', much of what constitutes public interest or what is private is left to the discretion of the media.

India is still at a very early stage of developing personal data protection. At present India does not provide significant protection to personal data in relation to all or most of the common privacy principles, in any sector, to meet any international standards.

Rights create a vacuum in which people can act however they choose. For there to be a "right" to privacy, then, there must be a vacuum in which privacy is unprotected, but in which privacy can be protected by people who value it. Non-protection of privacy has to be the default if we are to treat privacy as a right. Otherwise, privacy is an entitlement a thing that government bestows on us by virtue of our status. In the better view, privacy is the result of choices made in the exercise of some other right.

I feel that privacy is a right that shall be accorded to everyone regardless of their image, no matter what, so that instances like N.D.Tewari, Manu Singhvi, Sonia Gandhi etc be avoided to the extent it is feasible.

I would like to conclude with a quotation which I feel clearly states what I have tried to put through this book.

"Privacy is a protection from the unreasonable use of state and corporate power. But that is, in a sense, a secondary thing. In the first instance, privacy is the statement in words of a simple understanding, which belongs to the instinctive world rather than the formal one, that some things are the province of those who experience them and not naturally open to the scrutiny of others: courtship and love, with their emotional nakedness; the simple moments of family life; the appalling rawness of grief. That the state and other systems are precluded from snooping on these things is important - it is a strong barrier between the formal world and the hearth, extended or not - but at root privacy is a simple understanding: not everything belongs to everyone."

— **Nick Harkaway**

"Lastly one of my own"

"Privacy is the right which enables us to keep our lives free of unwanted speculation at our own cost and insistence and the authority to conceal the fact which we do not want the one's around us to know. Privacy is not something that I'm merely entitled to, it is something I am born with, it is in my words, an absolute prerequisite of every human being."

-Gaurav Goyal

BIBLIOGRAPHY

<u>Books</u>

1. G.Mishra, "Right to Privacy, Preeti Publications (Delhi) April (1994)

2. Radhabinod Pal, History of Hindu Law, Calcutta University Press, (1958)

3. Edward Shils, "Privacy: Its Constitution and Vicissitudes", Law and Contemporary Problems 31, No. 2 (Spring 1966).

4. KailashRai "Constitutional Law of India", Central Law Publications, (2001)

5. Prof. M.P. Jain, "Constitutional Law of India", Wadhwa and Company Nagpur, (2007)

6. Pandey, J.N., Constitutional Law of India, Central Law Agency (Allahabad) 43rd Edition (2006).

7. Geoffrey Robertson, QC and Andrew Nicol, Media Law, Penguin, 4th Edition (2009)

Other books

1. Alan F. Westin, Privacy and Freedom, 8. Atheneum New York 1970 Sixth Printing;

2. Adam Carlyle Breckenridge: The Right to Privacy, 1971. (Cited from Westlaw legal database);

3. Richard P. Claude (ed). Comparitive Human Rights;

4. V.R.Krishna Iyer, Justice and Beyond.

List of cases

1. Gokul Prasad v. Radho ILR 10 All. (1888) 358;

2. Manishankar Hargovan v. Trikam Narsi 5 Bom. H.C.R. (1876) ACJ 42;

3. Keshva Harkha v. ganpat Hira chand case 8 Bom H.C.Rep (1871) ACJ 87;

4. Sreenath Dutta v. Nand Kishore Bose 5 B.L.R. (1870) 676, 14 WR 103;

5. M.P.Sharma v. Satish Chandra, AIR 1954 SC 300 at 306-307;

6. Golak Prasad v. Radho, ILR 10 All. 358 at 388;

7. Kharak Singh v. State of Uttar Pradesh (1964) SCR (1) 332;

8. Govind v. State of Madhya Pradesh (AIR 1975 SC 1378);

9. R. Rajagopal v. State of Tamil Nadu (1994 SCC (6) 632);

10. Mohini Jain v. State of Karnataka AIR 1992 SC 1858;

11. Albert v. Strange (1849) 1 Mac & G 25 : 41 ER 1171 ;

12. Kaye v. Robertson. (1991) FSR 62;

13. Griswold v. Connecticut 381 US 479 (1965) ;

14. Roe v. Wade 410 US 113 (1973);

15. NAACP v. Alabama 377 US 288, 307 (1964) ;

16. Doe v. Borough of Barrington 729 F.Supp. 376 (D.N.J.,1990);

17. Whalen v. Roe, 429 U.S. 589, 599-600 (1977);

18. Chizmar v. Mackie, 896 P.2d 196 (Alaska 1995);

19. MacDonald v. Clinger, 446 N.Y.S.2d 801;

20. R. Rajagopal v. State of T.N. (1994) 6 SCC 632 ;

21. State of Maharashtra v. Madhulkar Narain AIR 1991 SC 207;

22. All India Imam Organization v. Union of India, AIR 1993 SC 2086;

23. Mr. 'X' v. Hospital 'Z' AIR 1999 SC 495;

24. Ms X v. Mr. Z, (1998) 8 SCC 296;

25. Surjit Singh Thind v. Kanwaljit KaurAIR 2003 P H 353;

26. Malak Singh v. State of Punjab, AIR 1981 SC 760;

27. State of Maharashtra v. Prabhakar Pandurang, AIR 1986 SC 424;

28. M.P. Sharma v. Statish Chandra, AIR 1954 SC 300;

29. Kharak Singh v. State of U. P. AIR 1963 SC 1295;

30. Wolf v. Colorado, (1948) 338 US 25;

31. Gobind v. State of M.P. AIR 1975 SC 1378;

32. Olmstead v.United States 277 U.S. 438 (1928);

33. State of Punjab v. Gurmit Singh AIR 1996 SC 1393;

34. Neera Mathur v. Life Insurance Corporation of India (1992) 1 SCC 286;

35. Nihal Chand v. Bhagwan Dei AIR 1935 All 1002;

36. R. M. Malkani v. State of Maharashtra AIR 1973 SC 157;

37. Peoples Union for Civil Liberties v. Union of India 1995 SCALE (2) 542;

38. LIC of India v. Consumer Education & Research Centre, (1995) 5 SCC 482;

39. Pragati Varghese v. Cyril George Varghese AIR 1997 Bom. 349;

40. T. Sareetha v. T. VenkataSubbaih AIR 1983 AP 356;

41. Harvinder Kaur v. Harminder Singh AIR 1984 Del 66

42. Saroj Rani v. Sudarshan Kumar AIR 1984 SC 1562

43. Sharda v. Dharampal AIR 2003 SC 3450

44. Kamalanantha And Ors vs State Of Tamil Nadu Appeal (crl.) 611-612 of 2003

45. Sharda vs Dharmpal AIR 2003 SC 3450

46. The State Of Bombay vs Kathi Kalu Oghad 1962 SCR (3) 10

47. Mascon Global Limited V. CCA, Google

48. http://www.mit.gov.in/sites/uploadfiles/dit/files/appeal/ (last visited on Nov. 21,2012)

49. Ram Jethmalani vs Union of India, 2011 No equivalent citation found

50. Mr.S.Rajamohan v Bsnl, Chennai, (2009), CIC/AD/A/X/09/00129

51. Ms. Kanchan Vora v Union Bank Of India, (2008), http://indiankanoon.org/doc/456808/

52. Shri P. Thavasiraj v Dept. Of Atomic Energy, (2008),

53. http://indiankanoon.org/doc/1718696/

54. K.P. Subhashchandran v National Aviation Company, (2008),

55. http://indiankanoon.org/doc/1067875/

56. Mrs.Shobha R. Arora v. Income Tax (2006), Mumbai, Ms. Neeru Bajaj Vs. Income Tax (2007), Bimal Kanti

57. Datta v Income Tax Department, (2008), http://indiankanoon.org/doc/292462/

58. Shri.Chetan Kothari vs Bhabha Atomic Research Centre (2011),

59. http://indiankanoon.org/doc/425930/

60. Vinod Kaushik v. Madhvika Joshi, (2011),

61. http://catindia.gov.in/pdfFiles/Appeal_No_2.pdf (last visited Nov 23, 2012).

62. Shruti Singh Chauhan v Directorate Of Vigilance, (2008),

63. http://indiankanoon.org/doc/1128532/

64. Romesh Thapar Case AIR 1950 S.C. 124

65. Sakal papers, AIR 1962 S.C. 305

66. Hamdard Dawakhana v. Union of India, AIR 1960 S.C. 554

67. Uma Khurana WP(Crl.) No.1175/2007

Journals

1. Goffman, "Presentation of Self"

2. Samuel D. Warren and Lois Brandeis, "The Right to Privacy," 4 Harvard Law Review, 193 (1980)

3. Charles fried, "Privacy", 77 Yale Law Journal (1965) 475, 482-483

4. Prashant Iyengar, Privacy and the Information Technology Act in India, SSRN ELIBRARY (2011)

5. Mubarak Ansari, Estranged wife hacks man's email, SAKAL TIMES, August 25, 2011

6. Usha Ramanthan, A Unique Identity Bill, Economic and Political Weekly, 10-14 (2010).

7. Ravi Shukla, Reimagining Citizenship: Debating India's Unique Identification Scheme, Economic and Political Weekly, 31-36 (2010)

8. Sheetal Asrani-Dann, The Right to Privacy in the Era of Smart Governance: Concerns Raised By the Introduction of Biomet Immanuel Kant (Translated by Herbert James Paton) The moral law: groundwork of the metaphysic of morals, 42 (2005)

9. Immanuel Kant (Translated by Herbert James Paton) The moral law: groundwork of the metaphysic of morals, 42 (2005)

10. Shuddharbrata Sengupta, Every Day Surveillance in Sarai Reader 2002: The Cities of Everyday Life, 297-301 (2002)

11. Theodore F. Claypoole:- "Privacy Regulations a Concern with Internet" LexisNexis Martindale-Hubbell (R) Legal Articles

12. Anoop MS (2007). Public key Cryptography - Applications Algorithms and Mathematical Explanations. India: Tata Elxsi.

Conference Reports

22-23 May, 1967, StockHolm, Organised by the Swedish section of the International "Commission of Jurists"; 30 September- 3 October 1970, Brussels, France and Switzerland

Dictionary

Black's Law Dictionary, (9th Ed., 2009)

Websites

1. www.manupatra.com

2. www.lexisnexis.com

3. www.westlaw.com

4. www.papers.ssrn.com

5. www.mit.gov.in

6. www.sakaaltimes.com

7. www.ndtv.com

8. www.hindustantimes.com

9. www.psrindia.org

10. www.indiankanoon.org

URLS

1. http://papers.ssrn.com/sol3/papers.cfm?abstract_id =1807575 (last visited Nov. 22, 2012)

2. http://www.mit.gov.in/sites/upload_files/dit/ files/GSR3_10511%281%29.pdf (last accessed November 15th, 2011)

3. http://www.mit.gov.in/sites/uploadfiles/dit/files/ appeal/ (last visited on Nov. 21,2012)

4. http://www.sakaaltimes.com/ sakaaltimesbeta/20110825/4640115296625293785. htm (last visited Oct 3, 2011).

5. http://cyberpolicebangalore.nic.in/pdf/notification _1.pdf

6. http://www.ndtv.com/article/india/high-court-dismisses-appeal-seeking-information-on-sonia-gandhi-s-religion-69356

7. http://www.psrindia.org/uploads/media//NIA%20 Draft%20Bill.pdf

8. http://ncrb.nic.in/CII-2009-NEW/Compendium 2009.pdf (last visited Nov. 23, 2012)

Statutes

1. The Information Technology (Reasonable security practices and procedures and sensitive personal information) Rules, 2011.

2. The Information Technology Act, 2008

3. CONSTITUTION OF INDIA, 1950

4. INTERNATIONAL COVENANT ON CIVIL AND POLITICAL RIGHTS

5. UNIVERSAL DECLARATION OF HUMAN RIGHTS

6. Privacy Bill, 2011